American
English in Mind

Herbert Puchta & Jeff Stranks

Workbook Starter

CAMBRIDGE
UNIVERSITY PRESS

CAMBRIDGE UNIVERSITY PRESS
Cambridge, New York, Melbourne, Madrid, Cape Town, Singapore,
São Paulo, Delhi, Dubai, Tokyo, Mexico City

Cambridge University Press
32 Avenue of the Americas, New York, NY 10013-2473, USA

www.cambridge.org
Information on this title: www.cambridge.org/9780521733298

© Cambridge University Press 2011

First published 2011

Printed in Hong Kong, China, by Sheck Wah Tong Printing Press Limited

A catalog record for this publication is available from the British Library.

ISBN 978-0-521-73323-6 Student's Book Starter
ISBN 978-0-521-73324-3 Starter Combo A
ISBN 978-0-521-73325-0 Starter Combo B
ISBN 978-0-521-73329-8 Workbook Starter
ISBN 978-0-521-73330-4 Teacher's Edition Starter
ISBN 978-0-521-73331-1 Class Audio Starter
ISBN 978-0-521-73326-7 Classware Starter
ISBN 978-0-521-73332-8 Testmaker Starter
ISBN 978-0-521-73343-4 DVD Starter

Art direction, book design and layout: Pentacor plc
Photo research: Pronk and Associates

Contents

1 The world around me

1 Remember and check

Are the people saying *hello* or *goodbye*? Write *hello* or *goodbye* on the line.
Then check page 2 of the Student's Book.

1 Hey, Steve.   _hello_
2 Hi, Joanne.   _____
3 Well, goodbye. _____
4 Hello, Mrs. Jackson. _____
5 See you later. _____
6 Yeah, see you. _____

2 Vocabulary

✳ The day

Complete the conversations with the correct words.

> night   morning   evening   afternoon

Ruben: Good _____, Ms. Vega.
Ms. Vega: Hi, Ruben. How are you?
Ruben: Fine, thanks.

Mr. and Mrs. Hall: Good _____ .
Mr. and Mrs. Mora: Goodbye, and thanks.
Mr. and Mrs. Hall: You're welcome. Bye.

Tim: Uh, hi, Mom. Hi, Dad.
Mom: Well, good _____, Tim. How are you today?
Tim: Mmm. I'm OK.

Waiter: Good _____ . Two for dinner?
Man: Yes, please.
Waiter: Fine.

✱ International words

a ▶ **CD3 T08** Listen and write the numbers 1–6 in the boxes.

b ▶ **CD3 T08** Listen again and write the words. Then check the words in the box on page 4 of the Student's Book.

----------------------- -----------------------

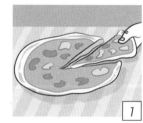

----------------------- -----------------------

[1]

----------------------- -----------------------

c Write the words in the chart.

<del>airport</del> bus café hamburger hotel
museum pizza sandwich taxi

Places in the city	Transportation	Food
airport		

d What other international words do you know? Write them here.

computer ---------------- ----------------

---------------- ---------------- ----------------

---------------- ---------------- ----------------

---------------- ---------------- ----------------

---------------- ---------------- ----------------

✱ Classroom objects

What are the words? Match the words with the picture. Write the words in the blanks.

pne abdro lepnic tonbokeo
<del>nowwid</del> sked richa rodo

1 _window_
2 ----------------
3 ----------------
4 ----------------
5 ----------------
6 ----------------
7 ----------------
8 ----------------

3 Grammar review

✱ Regular plural nouns

a Look at these examples of singular and plural nouns.

door	doors
phone	phones
sandwich	sandwiches
desk	desks

b Complete the table.

Singular	Plural
hotel	*hotels*
page	
notebook	
watch	
taxi	
bus	
pencil	
chair	

✱ Irregular plural nouns

c Write the numbers and the plural form of the words.

child   woman   person   man

1 _____*four men*_____   2 _____

3 _____   4 _____

d Complete the sentences. Write the words.

child   children   man   ~~men~~
woman   women

1 Mr. Ozawa and Mr. Hill are _____*men*_____ .

2 Ms. Hunter is a _____ .

3 Mr. Clinton is a _____ .

4 Susie is three. She's a _____ .

5 Tim and Sam are two. They're _____ .

6 Ms. Turner and Mrs. Russo are _____ .

4 Listen

▶ **CD3 T09** Listen. (Circle) the words you hear.

1	book	(books)
2	door	doors
3	page	pages
4	woman	women
5	desk	desks
6	hamburger	hamburgers
7	airport	airports
8	sandwich	sandwiches

5 Pronunciation

✱ Syllables

▶ **CD3 T10** Listen. How many syllables are there in these words? Write the number.

1	window	*2*
2	chair	
3	women	
4	sandwiches	
5	museum	
6	buses	
7	music	
8	board	
9	pages	
10	computer	

6 Culture in mind

Write the words under the pictures.

bow   handshake   Hi, how are you?   high five   hug   wave

1 _____*Hi, how are you?*_____

2 _____

3 _____

4 _____

5 _____

6 _____

7 Study help

✱ Vocabulary

Look and listen for English words in the world around you. (Circle) words you know in these examples.

- English newspapers and magazines

U.S. PRESIDENT ARRIVES IN TOKYO TODAY

- English words on menus in restaurants

Sandwiches

Tuna salad

Chicken

Cheese and tomato

- Television and movies

Hello, kids!
And how are you this evening?

Skills in mind

8 Listen

▶ **CD3 T11** Listen to the conversations. What are the people talking about? (Circle) the correct answer.

1 (pencils)   pens   desks

2 the classroom   their friends   a museum

3 chickens   sandwiches   the café

4 vocabulary   the bookstore   notebooks

9 Write

Look around you. How many things can you name in English? Make a list.

two pencils

a notebook

a chair

...

LISTENING TIP

Understanding the main idea

You don't need to understand every word.

Listen for repeated words.

Ask: *What are the people talking about?*

Unit check

1 Fill in the blanks

Complete the conversations with the words in the box.

> hi   good   fine   how   ~~morning~~   night
> see   thank   thanks   this

Mr. Wilson: Good _morning_, Dennis.

Dennis: Hello, Mr. Wilson. [1]_____ are you today?

Mr. Wilson: I'm fine, [2]_____ you.

Tina: Good [3]_____, Jean.

Jean: Goodbye. [4]_____ you in the morning.

Tina: Yeah, see you.

Joe: [5]_____ evening, Mrs. Chan. How are you?

Mrs. Chan: I'm [6]_____. And you?

Joe: Oh, I'm OK.

Danny: Hi, Wendy. What's up?

Wendy: Hello, Danny. [7]_____ is my friend, Tom.

Danny: [8]_____, Tom. How are you?

Tom: Hi, Danny. I'm fine, [9]_____.

| | 9 |

2 Complete the table

Write the singular or plural forms.

Singular	Plural
book	*books*
	pages
watch	
	hamburgers
taxi	
pizza	
	sandwiches
teacher	
bus	

| | 8 |

3 Vocabulary

Write the words in the correct columns in the table.

> children   ~~desk~~   hotel   men   museum   notebook   pen   pizza   sandwich

In the classroom	In the city	In the restaurant	People
desk			

| | 8 |

How did you do?

Total: | 25 |

| | Very good
25 – 20 | | OK
19 – 16 | | Review Unit 1 again
15 or less |

1   Remember and check

What do you say? Match the sentences. Then check page 8 of the Student's Book.

1   You need help.   _f_   a   Excuse me ...

2   You want someone's attention. ....   b   You're welcome.

3   You don't understand something.   c   I don't understand.

4   You can't answer a question. ....   d   I can help you.

5   Someone needs help. ....   e   Please.

6   Someone gives you something. ....   f   Can you help me?

7   You ask for something. ....   g   Thank you.

8   Someone says, "Thank you" to you. ....   h   I'm sorry. I don't know.

2   Grammar review

✱ Adjectives

a   Look at the pictures. If the adjective is correct, write (✓). If the adjective is wrong, write the correct adjective.

small
1   a ~~big~~ restaurant

2   an expensive pen ✓

3   a new computer

4   an interesting book

5   a bad soccer team

6   a big hamburger

7   an old taxi

8   a good hotel

✱ a/an

b Write *a* or *an*.

1 The Model-T is __an__ old car.

2 Mimi is _____ bad cat.

3 *Beloved* is _____ good book.

4 The Desmond is _____ new hotel.

5 That's _____ expensive TV.

6 The White House is _____ big house.

7 Key West is _____ small city.

8 It's _____ interesting problem.

3 Spelling

✱ The alphabet

a ▶ **CD3 T12** Complete the alphabet. Write the letters. Then listen and say the letters.

A _____ _____ D _____ _____ _____

H _____ _____ K _____ M _____ O _____

Q _____ _____ _____ U _____

W _____ _____ and _____ .

b ▶ **CD3 T13** Listen to the spelling. Write the letters. What is the sentence?

Lu _____

_____

c ▶ **CD3 T14** Listen and write the words.

1 Name: Kevin _____

City: _____

2 Name: Julie _____

City: _____

4 Pronunciation

✱ Letter sounds

▶ **CD3 T15** Listen. Circle the letter you hear.

1 B Ⓥ

2 A E

3 E I

4 G J

5 B P

6 D T

7 K Q

8 S Z

5 Vocabulary

✱ Colors

Look at the pictures and complete numbers 1–6 in the puzzle with the colors. What is the color in number 7?

¹G	R	A	⁷Y		
			²		
			³		
			⁴		
	⁵				
			⁶		

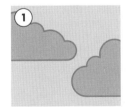
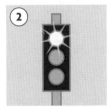

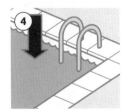
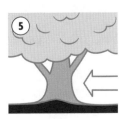

7 _____

✱ Numbers 0–20

a Write the missing words for the numbers.

1 one   two   three   ....

2 ....   seven   ....   nine   ....

3 eleven   ....   thirteen   ....

4 ....   seventeen   ....   nineteen   ....

b Write the answers.

1 nine + nine   = *eighteen*

2 four + seven   = ...

3 two + twelve   = ...

4 one + eight   = ...

5 three + two   = ...

6 twelve + eight   = ...

7 ten + seven   = ...

8 four + eight   = ...

✱ Numbers 20–100

a Write the next two numbers.

1 ten   thirty   fifty   *seventy*   ....

2 four   eight   sixteen   ....

3 three   six   twelve   ....

4 forty-one   fifty-two   sixty-three   ....

5 eighty-four   eighty-one   seventy-eight   ....

6 twenty-nine   thirty-three   thirty-seven   ....

b ▶ **CD3 T16** Listen and (circle) the numbers you hear.

1 ⑬ / 30   hotels

2 15 / 50   DVDs

3 17 / 70   pencils

4 14 / 40   chairs

5 16 / 60   women

6 18 / 80   pages

c Read the message. Then complete the conversations with the words for the numbers.

Message from Amanda –

The math homework is on page 87.

She needs help.

Please call 212-216-1905.

Mom: Oh, here's a message for you. It's from Amanda.

You: Oh, yes?

Mom: Yes, she says the math homework is on page ....
Please call her.

You: What's her phone number?

Mom: It's .... – .... – ....

6 Everyday English

Complete the conversations with the correct expression.

| busy | call me | What | What's this |

1 A: _____ ?

  B: Hmm... I don't know. Is it a pen?

2 A: Good morning, Michael!

  B: Please, _____ Mike. That's my nickname.

3 A: Hello, I'm Jeremiah Cook.

  B: Sorry. I don't understand. *Jer* – _____ ?

  A: Jeremiah.

4 A: Sorry. I can't help you now. I'm _____ .

  B: That's OK. I'll see you later.

7 Study help

✱ Alphabetical order

Sometimes it's a good idea to put words or names in alphabetical order. Then it's easy to find the word. Dictionaries and telephone books use alphabetical order.

a Complete the list with words in the box. Use alphabetical order. If two words begin with the same letter, use the second letter: for example black comes before brown.

| desk | pencil | book | door | ~~board~~ | ~~computer~~ | ~~notebook~~ | ~~window~~ |

Things in the classroom

board _____ _____

computer _____ _____ _____

notebook _____ _____

window _____

b Write the international words in alphabetical order.

| museum | hamburger | taxi | phone | bus | hotel | ~~airport~~ |
| pizza | sandwich | restaurant | café | international |

_____ *airport* _____ _____

_____ _____

_____ _____

_____ _____

_____ _____

_____

c Make a list of your friends' names and phone numbers. Write the names along with the numbers in alphabetical order.

8 Read

Read the signs. Where are they? Write the place under the picture.

hotel   museum   ~~taxi~~   airport   bus   restaurant

1

FARE

$2.50	**INITIAL CHARGE**
40¢	Per 1/5 mile
40¢	Per 2 minutes stopped
50¢	Extra night charge
	8 p.m. – 6 a.m.

taxi

2

Full fare:	**$2.25**
Seniors:	$1.10
Students with Student MetroCard:	Free
Children under 44" with adult:	Free

3

- 💼 Baggage Claim
- 💳 Ticketing/Check in
- $ ATM
- ✈ Terminals 1 2 3 4

→

4

Shhh!
Please
Do Not
Disturb

5

Harvest Home

Lunch: Tuesday – Sunday: 11:30 a.m. to 2:30 p.m.

Dinner: Tuesday – Saturday: 5:30 to 11:00 p.m.

Sunday: 4:00 to 9:00 p.m.

6

PLEASE
DO NOT TOUCH
THE PAINTINGS

READING TIP

Start reading

Reading is a good way to learn more English quickly. Try these ideas.

- Look for signs in different languages. Read the sign in your language. Then read the sign in English.

- Read easy stories in English. For example, read children's stories that you already know.

- Look at pictures in English magazines and newspapers. Then read the words under the pictures.

- Read English labels on things in the supermarket or other stores.

Unit check

1 Fill in the blanks

Complete the conversations with the words in the box.

> address   color   don't know
> don't understand   excuse me
> ~~mean~~   phone number   problem
> thank you   welcome

1   **Ms. James:** Kim, What does *baggage* ___mean___ ?

   Kim: Sorry, Ms. James. I _____ .

2   **Kate:** I _____ the homework.

   Jean: That's OK. I can help you.

   Kate: Thanks, Jean.

   Jean: You're _____ .

3   **Paul:** _____ , Ms. James.

   Ms. James: Yes, Paul.

   Paul: What's your favorite _____ ?

   Ms. James: It's yellow.

4   **Marvin:** Ramón, what's your _____ ?

   Ramón: It's 213-555-7894.

   Marvin: And what's your _____ .

   Ramón: It's 73 Fourth Avenue.

   Marvin: _____ .

   Ramón: No _____ .

| 9 |

2 Choose the correct answers

Circle the correct answer: a, b or c.

1   Guadalajara is _____ big city.

   a an   b it   c a *(c circled)*

2   That's _____ interesting idea.

   a an   b and   c a

3   I have _____ pen.

   a an   b blue   c a

4   It's _____ .

   a yellow the taxi   b a taxi yellow
   c a yellow taxi

5   It's _____ .

   a a old book   b an old book   c a book old

6   A: I can help you.   B: _____ .

   a Thank   b Thanks   c Thanks you

7   The opposite of *interesting* is _____ .

   a *good*   b *boring*   c *old*

8   The opposite of *old* is _____ .

   a *new*   b *child*   c *bad*

9   The opposite of *expensive* is _____ .

   a *cheap*   b *small*   c *bad*

| 8 |

3 Vocabulary

Write the words for the numbers.

1	_twenty-eight_	28	4	_____	67	7	_____	79
2	_____	94	5	_____	45	8	_____	0
3	_____	32	6	_____	83	9	_____	51

| 8 |

How did you do?

Total: | 25 |

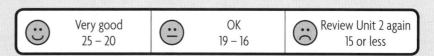

| 😊 | Very good 25 – 20 | 😐 | OK 19 – 16 | 🙁 | Review Unit 2 again 15 or less |

3 He's a soccer player.

1 Grammar

✱ The verb *be* (singular)

a Match the sentences in 1b with the pictures. Write numbers 1–7 in the boxes.

b Look at the underlined words. Write the short form, with *'m*, *'s* or *'re*.

1 <u>It is</u> a boring movie.

..............*It's*..............

2 <u>She is</u> an excellent singer.

....

3 <u>You are</u> a great teacher.

....

4 <u>It is</u> a new computer game.

....

5 <u>Richard is</u> from New York City.

....

6 <u>Australia is</u> a big country.

....

7 <u>I am</u> Carla. <u>What is</u> your name?

....

c Complete the dialogues.

1 A: Is Dinara Safina a movie star?

   B: No, _she's_ a tennis player.

2 A: Ashton Kutcher is an English actor, I think.

   B: No, he isn't . ... from the U.S.

3 A: Is this DVD good?

   B: Yes, ... great!

4 A: I think .... from Britain.

   B: No, I'm not. I'm American.

5 A: What's *puerta* in English?

   B: .... "door."

A

B

C

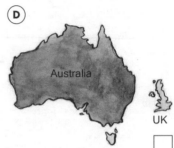

D

Australia

UK

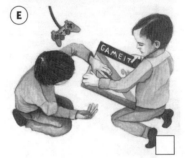

E

F

7

G

d Write the negative forms in the table.

Affirmative	Negative – full forms	Negative – short forms
1 I am	*I am not*	*I'm not*
2 You are		
3 He is		
4 She is		
5 It is		

e Write affirmative or negative sentences.

1 he / a singer

He isn't a singer.

2 she / British

She's British.

3 it / Japanese

_____

4 she / the winner

_____

5 it / boring

_____

6 you / a movie star

_____

7 it / expensive

_____

8 you / a bad dog

_____

f Put the words in order to make questions.

1 you/OK/Are

Are you OK? _____

2 Mexican/she/Is

_____

3 Madrid/you/Are/from

_____

4 right/I/Am

_____

5 big/a/Is/it/city

_____

6 Brad/Pitt/good/a/actor/Is

_____

g ▶ **CD3 T17** Write the questions. Then listen, check and repeat.

1 She's American.

Is she American? _____

2 You're from Japan.

_____

3 He's a good teacher.

_____

4 It's a cheap restaurant.

_____

5 I'm the winner!

_____

6 Broadway's in New York.

_____

7 The hotel's expensive.

_____

8 Maria's from Spain.

_____

9 You're a singer.

_____

10 The answer's on page 5.

_____

2 Vocabulary

✱ Countries

a Write the names of the countries on the map.

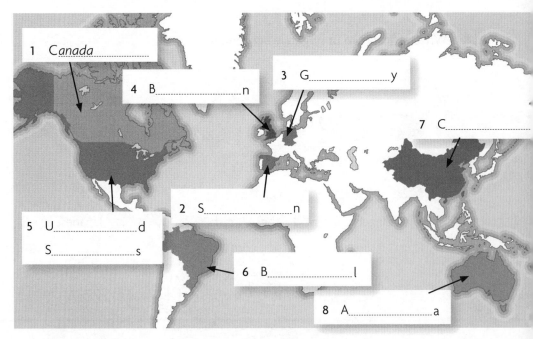

1 Canada
3 G_____y
4 B_____n
7 C_____
2 S_____n
5 U_____d
  S_____s
6 B_____l
8 A_____a

✱ Nationalities

b Find eight nationalities in the word search.

I	T	A	A	L	L	B	A	R	H	T
T	U	R	M	G	E	R	M	A	N	I
A	R	C	E	F	T	I	O	I	A	N
M	L	S	X	A	T	T	A	L	S	C
E	D	P	I	K	W	I	S	J	T	A
R	H	A	C	W	I	S	T	P	V	N
I	S	N	A	A	S	H	R	A	I	A
C	H	I	N	E	S	E	G	L	O	D
A	U	S	T	R	A	L	I	A	N	I
N	X	H	A	M	E	R	A	D	Z	A
A	M	B	R	A	Z	I	L	I	A	N

d **Vocabulary bank** Find the country names. Write them and add the nationalities.

1 ECFRNA   _France / French_

2 KURTEY   _____

3 TIRGANENA   _____

4 GOLTRAPU   _____

5 WINTERSLADZ   _____

6 CEEGER   _____

7 DARLINE   _____

8 AAILTHND   _____

c Where are they from? Write two sentences about each person.

1 _He's from Brazil._   2 _____
  He's Brazilian.   _____

3 _____   4 _____

5 _____   6 _____

3 Pronunciation

✱ from

▶ **CD3 T18** Listen. ⊙Circle the word *from* when it's stressed.

1 Where's he ⊙from? He's from Switzerland.

2 Are you from Sweden? No, I'm from Australia.

3 Where are you from? I'm from Italy.

4 Where's she from? She's from Morocco.

4 Grammar

✱ *wh-* question words

a Match the questions and answers.

1 What's your name?   a He's OK.
2 Who's she?   b Kate.
3 How are you?   c I'm fine, thanks.
4 How's Nick?   d Mr. Jones.
5 Where are you from?   e I don't know.
6 Who's your English teacher?   f Turkey.

b Complete the sentences. Use *Who, Where, What* or *How.*

1 I don't know her. __Who__ is she?
2 _____'s your phone number?
3 _____ are you from?
4 _____'s the name of the hotel?
5 A: _____'s Sydney?
   B: It's in Australia.
6 A: _____'s that girl?
   B: My friend Sally.
7 _____ old is she?
8 A: _____'s this?
   B: It's my vocabulary notebook.

5 Culture in mind

Look at the pictures and complete the sentences.

Armando

BRAZIL
São Paulo

1 Armando's a _soccer player_ . He's from _____ . He's _____ .

Alicia

MEXICO
Veracruz

2 Alicia's a _____ . She's from _____ . She's _____ .

Wei

Beijing
CHINA

3 Wei's a _____ . He's from _____ . He's _____ .

6 Study help

✱ Vocabulary

a For every unit, write new words in your Vocabulary notebook. Write them in groups. For example:

Classroom things	Classroom verbs
desk	*listen*
board	*read*
pen	

b Write these words in the lists.

pencil write look at chair notebook
say ask table match

c Look at the words in Unit 3 of your Student's Book. Write all the words you can find for these groups in the lists. Don't forget to look in the Vocabulary Bank on page 98, too!

Countries	Nationalities	Jobs
Italy	*Italian*	*actor*
Spain		
China		

Skills in mind

7 Read

Read the text. Then write *T* (true) or *F* (false).

I'm Jenny. I'm 14, and I'm American. My home is in St. Augustine, Florida. It's an old city, but it isn't very big. My address is 384 Bridge Street, and my phone number is 904-555-6520.

My best friend is Ricardo. He's from Peru, but his father is Japanese. Ricardo is 15, so he isn't in my class at school. He isn't a very good basketball player, but I think he's a great singer. He's a good friend, and he helps me with my homework.

1   The girl's name is Jenny.   `T`

2   She's from the United States.   ☐

3   St. Augustine is a new city.   ☐

4   It's a small city.   ☐

5   Ricardo is Jenny's friend.   ☐

6   Ricardo is French.   ☐

7   He isn't in Jenny's class.   ☐

8   He's a great basketball player.   ☐

READING TIP

New words

What happens if you don't know a word in a reading text?

- You can understand the text even if you don't know all the words.

- Look at the word. Is it similar to a word in your language?

- Look at the other words in the sentence and think about the new word. Can you guess the meaning?

8 Write

Complete the interview with Jenny. Write one word in each space.

Interviewer: Where [1]_____ [2]_____ from?

Jenny: [3]_____ from St. Augustine. It's a [4]_____ in Florida.

Interviewer: [5]_____ it a big city?

Jenny: [6]_____ , it [7]_____ .

Interviewer: [8]_____ your [9]_____?

Jenny: It's 384 Bridge Street.

Interviewer: I know Ricardo's your [10]_____ friend. Is [11]_____ Peruvian?

Jenny: Yes, [12]_____ [13]_____ .

Interviewer: [14]_____ old [15]_____ he?

Jenny: [16]_____ 15.

Unit check

1 Fill in the blanks

Complete the dialogues with the words in the box.

| Is   Italian   actor   from   Who's   teacher   ~~What's~~   is   Brazil   isn't |

1 A: Hello. ___What's___ your name?

   B: I'm Fabio and I'm from [1] _____ . This [2] _____ my friend Sonia.

   A: Is she [3] _____ Argentina?

   B: No, she [4] _____ . She's [5] _____ .

2 A: [6] _____ this?

   B: He's Luc Duval.

   A: [7] _____ he an [8] _____ ?

   B: No, he's a [9] _____ .

   9

2 Choose the correct answers

(Circle) the correct answer: a, b or c.

1 I think he's great! He's my _____ .

   a (hero)   b singer   c winner

2 She's a famous movie _____ .

   a player   b actress   c model

3 Ricardo's nationality is _____ .

   a Switzerland   b Spain   c Swiss

4 How old _____ ?

   a she is   b she's   c is she

5 _____ is a big country.

   a Canada   b French   c Chinese

6 This tennis player _____ Australian.

   a are   b aren't   c isn't

7 _____ are you from?

   a What   b Where   c How

8 Is _____ a Japanese flag?

   a he   b she   c it

9 _____ your address?

   a What's   b Who's   c Where's   **8**

3 Vocabulary

Underline the correct word in each sentence.

1 My friend lives in Tokyo. That's in _Japanese / Japan_.

2 Pedro speaks Spanish. He's _Colombia / Colombian_.

3 People in some parts of _Canadian / Canada_ speak English and French.

4 I think _China / Chinese_ is a difficult language.

5 She's from Brazil. She speaks _Portugal / Portuguese_.

6 I love going to Athens. _Greece / Greek_ food is very good.

7 Is this the _Germany / German_ flag?

8 _Irish / Ireland_ is beautiful. It's very green.

9 She's from Bangkok. That's in _Thai / Thailand_.   **8**

How did you do?

Total: **25**

 Very good 25 – 20   OK 19 – 16    Review Unit 3 again 15 or less

4 We're a new band.

1 Remember and check

Match the two parts of the sentences, and write the name of the speaker, *Sandra, Keith, Chuck* or *AM* (audience member). Check with the dialogue on page 22 of the Student's Book.

1 _Chuck_ This is ─────────── a a new band.

2 ─────────── The Targets are b are you?

3 ─────────── Chuck and I c our first song for you today.

4 ─────────── I'm d the same city?

5 ─────────── How old e are 19.

6 ─────────── Are you all from f from New York City.

2 Grammar

✱ The verb *be*: plural, negatives and questions

a Look at the pictures and complete the sentences.

1 _I'm_ a tennis player.

2 ─────────── my favorite singer.

3 I think ─────────── Australian.

4 What's that in English?
   ─────────── a notebook.

5 ─────────── from Peru.

6 ─────────── the winners.

7 ─────────── fantastic!

8 ─────────── boring.

b Write true sentences with the verb *be*.

1 Justin Bieber / American _Justin Bieber isn't American. He's Canadian._

2 Fernando Alonso / race car driver _Fernando Alonso is a race car driver._

3 Tokyo / city in China ───────────────────────────

4 My favorite restaurant / expensive ───────────────────────────

5 I / American ───────────────────────────

6 Ferrari cars / cheap ───────────────────────────

7 Daniel Radcliffe / actor ───────────────────────────

8 We / in Vancouver ───────────────────────────

c Match the questions and answers.

1　Is he Colombian?
2　Are they a Brazilian band?
3　Is this CD expensive?
4　Are you and John swimmers?
5　Are you from Korea?
6　Are Ann and Sophie good singers?
7　Am I a good tennis player?
8　Is she your friend?

a　No, she isn't. I don't know her.
b　No, it isn't. It's pretty cheap.
c　Yes, I think you are.
d　Yes, he is. He's from Cali.
e　No, they aren't. They're from Spain.
f　No, I'm not. I'm Japanese.
g　Yes, we are. We're on the school team.
h　Yes, they are. They're great.

d Write the questions.

1　Maria / from Bogotá?
　　Is Maria from Bogotá?

2　Ken and Sandy / American?

3　I / a good singer?

4　Where / you from, Sarah?

5　the movie / interesting?

6　you and Robert / basketball players?

7　Luis Miguel / popular in Mexico?

8　Julie and I / good actors?

9　Who / you?

10　What / your phone number?

e Read the questions and write true answers.

1　Are you a teacher?
　　No, I'm not. I'm a student.

2　Are you a good singer?

3　Are you from New York City?

4　Are you and your friends in a band?

5　Are CDs expensive in your country?

6　Is your mother a tennis player?

7　Is your teacher American?

8　Is your school very big?

✱ *I (don't) like … / Do you like … ?*

f Complete the dialogue.

Kate:　Do _you like_ sports?

Ben:　Yes, I ¹_____ . I ²_____
　　　soccer and ³_____ .

Kate:　⁴_____ you _____ golf?

Ben:　⁵_____ , I _____ .
　　　It's boring! And I ⁶_____ volleyball
　　　either.

3 Vocabulary

★ Positive and negative adjectives

a Circle the correct word.

1 I don't like pizza. I think it's *awful / fantastic*.
2 I like this DVD. It's *boring / fantastic*.
3 Justin Timberlake is my favorite singer. He's *terrible / great*.
4 I don't want to listen to Greg's new band. I think they're *excellent / terrible*.

b Use the words in the box to write about the pictures.

I like …	I think it's	great	terrible
I really like …	I think they're	awful	boring
I don't like …		fantastic	

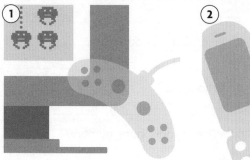
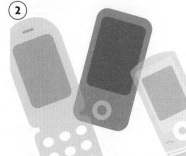

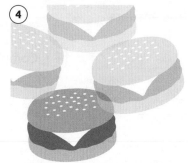

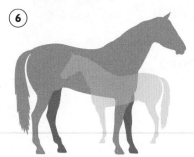

1 *I don't like computer games. I think they're boring.*
2 ....
3 ....
4 ....
5 ....
6 ....

c Vocabulary bank

Underline the correct word.

1 I love Tony's restaurant. Their tomato soup is *disgusting / delicious*.
2 This movie is *dreadful / wonderful*. I really don't like it.
3 He's a *dreadful / wonderful* soccer player. He scores a lot of goals.
4 This room is *disgusting / excellent*. Let's go to a different hotel.
5 He's good on the guitar, but as a singer he's *horrible / delicious*.
6 Read this book! It's *terrific / awful*.

4 Grammar

★ Object pronouns

Complete the sentences with object pronouns.

1 I don't like _____*her*_____ . She isn't very interesting.
2 Paul's a good singer. Listen to _____ .
3 Horses are great. I like _____ a lot.
4 Bye! See _____ on Friday!
5 Look! A picture of my favorite band! I want _____ !
6 I like Jim, but he doesn't like _____ .

5 Pronunciation

✱ /ɪ/ and /i/

a ▶ **CD3 T19** Listen to the underlined sounds. Write the words in the lists. Then listen again, check and repeat.

/ɪ/ is	/i/ three
think	see

see   think   singer   please
guitar   read   museum   city
CD   big   people   women

b ▶ **CD3 T20** Listen and repeat.

1 Three big museums.
2 We think he's Swiss.
3 Fifteen CDs, please.
4 The Italian singer is the winner.

6 Everyday English

Put the phrases in the box into the correct places.

Cool   Of course   I'm sorry   I know

1 A: Do you like this song?

   B: .... ! It's great!

2 A: Here. Have some ice cream!

   B: Oh, ... , Paula. I don't like ice cream.

3 A: Look! I have the new Lady Gaga CD.

   B: .... ! Let's listen to it now!

4 A: Queen Latifah isn't British.

   B: .... She's American.

7 Study help

✱ Pronunciation

Mark the stress on new words in your Vocabulary notebook like this:

● Underline the stressed syllable.

   fantastic   wonderful   favorite

● Put the mark ' in front of the stressed sound. This is the mark used in a dictionary.

   fan'tastic   'wonderful   'favorite

a Underline the stressed syllables in these words.

1 popular   5 computer
2 American   6 concert
3 Japanese   7 seventeen
4 terrible

b Write adjectives from Unit 4 in this list. Mark the stress.

   fan'tastic   ....

   ....

   ....

Skills in mind

8 Read and listen

a ▶ CD3 T21 Look at this girl's Internet homepage. Listen and complete the text. Write one word in each space.

Hi! Welcome to my homepage.

My name is **Sang-mi Park**. I live in San José in California, and I really like rock [1] _music_ . Can you guess who my [2] _____ rock stars are? No? Well, it's a new band called **The Answer!**

Here are **four things** I want to tell you about them.

- There are four people in the [3] _____ . **Cormac Neeson** is a singer. **Micky Waters** and **Paul Mahon** play guitar and bass, and **James Heatley** is the drummer.

- My favorite [4] _____ Cormac. I think he's [5] _____! And he's a [6] _____ singer!

- My favorite The Answer song is "Comfort Zone." All my friends say their favorite is "Never Too Late." (I think it's [7] _____ good, but it isn't my favorite.)

- The people in The Answer are all

[8] _____ Ireland, but they [9] _____ popular in Canada and the U.S., too. Their song "Never Too Late" is on the video game "Guitar Hero."

I hope you like The Answer, too.

LISTENING TIP

Before you listen

- Look at the pictures with the text. What is the topic of the text?
- Read the text before you listen.
- Try to guess the missing words. Write your ideas in pencil in the text.
- What <u>type</u> of word is it? Is it a noun (a person or thing)? Is it a verb (*is / are / go / like / listen ...*)? Is it an adjective (*popular / cheap / wonderful ...*)?

b Read the text again. Write *T* (true) or *F* (false).

1 Sang-mi is Australian. | F |
2 The Answer is Sang-mi's favorite band. | |
3 There are five people in the band. | |
4 Sang-mi likes the song "Comfort Zone." | |
5 Sang-mi thinks "Never Too Late" is a terrible song. | |
6 The people in The Answer are all from England. | |

Unit check

1 Fill in the blanks

Complete the sentences with the words in the box.

| wonderful | are | she's | together | ~~band~~ | aren't | we're | from | them | movie |

Mick, Keith and Carla are in a _____band_____ . Carla's ¹_____ Australia, and ²_____ the singer. The other two ³_____ from Canada. People don't know ⁴_____ in my country, so they ⁵_____ very popular here. But I think their music is ⁶_____ . They're in a new ⁷_____ now. My friend Elizabeth and I want to see it ⁸_____ , and ⁹_____ really excited. [9]

2 Choose the correct answers

(Circle) the correct answer: a, b or c.

1 Cathy's _____ about the concert.

   a fantastic   b popular   c (excited)

2 A: I want a sandwich. _____

   B: No, thanks. I'm OK.

   a Guess what?   b What about you?   c Let's go.

3 We don't like this CD. It's _____ .

   a favorite   b awful   c wonderful

4 Jan and Petra _____ from Germany.

   a is   b isn't   c aren't

5 A: Is she a good singer?

   B: Yes, we really like _____ .

   a us   b her   c him

6 _____ Brazilian?

   a You are   b Are you   c Do you

7 Lima _____ the capital of Colombia.

   a not   b isn't   c aren't

8 A: Do you like classical music?

   B: Yes, I _____ .

   a do   b is   c am

9 Listen to the words and repeat _____ .

   a it   b him   c them   [8]

3 Vocabulary

Find the adjectives. Complete the sentences.

1 Thanks for the present. It's _____great_____ (agrte).

2 Have a piece of this cake. It's _____ (odcielsiu).

3 She is a _____ (lwuofnrde) story teller. Let's go and listen to her.

4 Look, there are a lot of mice in the kitchen. It's _____ (dgigsutnis).

5 Don't ask me for help with French. My French is _____ (waluf).

6 I don't want to hear this song again! It's _____ (dfldreau).

7 I don't like this computer. It's _____ (rltebrie).

8 Thank you for the book. It's _____ (xteelnecl).

9 My favorite rock band is Arctic Monkeys. They're _____ (nattiasfc). [8]

How did you do?

| ☺ Very good 25 – 20 | ☺ OK 19 – 16 | ☹ Review Unit 4 again 15 or less |

Total: [25]

5 She lives in Washington.

1 Remember and check

Match the two parts of the sentences. Then check with the text on page 30 of the Student's Book.

1 Michelle Obama   a the White House in Washington, D.C.

2 Millions of people see   b important projects for the American people.

3 She lives in   c very busy.

4 Mrs. Obama's mother   d is American.

5 She's   e lives in the White House, too.

6 She works on   f her on TV.

2 Grammar

✱ Simple present: affirmative and negative

a Find 11 more verbs in the wordsnake. Write them under the pictures.

learn read work live play speak stop watch write study understand listen

① _____ ② _____ ③ _____

④ _____ ⑤ *learn* ⑥ _____

⑦ _____ ⑧ _____ ⑨ _____

⑩ _____ ⑪ _____ ⑫ _____

b Complete the sentences with the verb + *s*, *es* or *ies*.

1 She _____*likes*_____ the city. (like)

2 James _____ TV after school. (watch)

3 Sarah _____ to the park on Saturdays. (go)

4 He _____ German. (speak)

5 My father _____ to classical music. (listen)

6 School _____ at 3:30. (finish)

7 My friend _____ in a bookstore. (work)

8 Lisa _____ music at school. (study)

c Complete the sentences. Use the correct form of the verbs in the box.

speak   watch   ~~listen~~   understand   write   live   play

1 I _____*listen*_____ to pop music on the radio.
2 Rick Riordan _____ science fiction books.
3 My cousins _____ a lot of sports on TV.
4 We _____ volleyball at school.

5 My aunt _____ four languages.
6 You _____ in a big house!
7 I _____ the question, but I don't know the answer.

d Look at the pictures and write sentences.

1 Caroline / speak

   Caroline speaks Spanish, but she doesn't speak French.

2 Sam / like _____

3 Tony and Jill / watch _____
   _____

4 We / play _____
   _____

5 Julie / listen _____
   _____

✱ Simple present: questions and short answers

e Complete the sentences with *Do* or *Does*.

1 ___*Do*___ you like sports?
2 _____ Marcel live in Paris?
3 _____ your mother listen to music?
4 _____ Peter and Jack sometimes go to the museum?
5 _____ you play computer games at home?
6 _____ we know the answer to this question?
7 _____ your uncle use a cell phone?

f Write the questions. Then write true answers.

1 you / watch TV before school?

   Do you watch TV before school?
   Yes, I do.   or   *No, I don't.*

2 you / always finish your homework?
   _____
   _____

3 your best friend / like rap music?
   _____
   _____

4 you and your friends / play volleyball?
   _____
   _____

5 your teacher / speak English?
   _____
   _____

6 your friends / understand Italian?
   _____
   _____

3 Pronunciation

✳ /s/, /z/ and /ɪz/

▶ **CD3 T22** Listen and write the underlined sound: **/s/**, **/z/** or **/ɪz/**. Then listen again, check and repeat.

1 She likes it here. _/s/_
2 Does Anna study music? ....
3 Sam watches DVDs. ....
4 She writes a lot of letters. ....
5 He lives in Miami. ....
6 The class finishes soon. ....
7 Paul speaks Italian. ....

4 Vocabulary and grammar

✳ Family and possessive 's

a Look at the family tree and complete the sentences.

1 Rosa is Maria's _____mother_____ .
2 Barbara is Maria's _____ .
3 Maria's _____ are Steve and John.
4 Steve's _____ is Patricia.
5 Rosa is Barbara's _____ .
6 David is _____ uncle.
7 Sally's _____ are Maria's grandparents.
8 Matt is _____ father.
9 _____ sister is Sally.

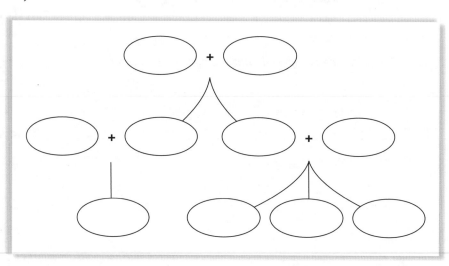

b Draw your family tree. In the ovals, write the family words and the people's names.

c Write five sentences about your family.

My father's name is David, and my mother's name is Rosa.
Steve and John are my brothers, and Barbara is …

----

d **Vocabulary bank** Complete the sentences with the correct words.

1 My mother's mother is my father's _mother-in-law_ .

2 My name's Paul. I'm my grandfather's
....

3 My name is Marianne. I'm my grandfather's
....

4 Paul and Marianne are their grandfather and grandmother's
....

5 My grandmother and my grandfather are my
....

6 My brother Tony's wife is Janet. Her father is Tony's
....

5 Grammar

✱ Possessive adjectives

<u>Underline</u> the correct words.

1 I play games on _my_ / I / me computer.

2 No problem! We can help you with you / your / our homework.

3 Dave lives in the U.S., but his / her / their grandparents live in Canada.

4 Amy watches he / she / her favorite basketball team on TV.

5 My friends and I like me / their / our new teacher.

6 The classroom is big, but its / his / their windows are small.

7 My aunt and uncle like pop music, but his / her / their children like rock.

6 Culture in mind

What are the words? Write them under the pictures. Then check with the text on page 34 of the Student's Book.

| usheo | ~~spearspewn~~ | runse | catyfor | signamaze | pentamart |

newspapers

7 Study help

✱ Vocabulary

a In your Vocabulary notebook, write words together. For example:

go	to the movies	speak	a language
	for a walk		French
	shopping		to my friend

b Write words that go with these verbs.

Verbs

work	_in a store_	write	
play		read	
watch		listen to	

8 Listen

▶ **CD3 T23**   Listen to Alice talking about her friend Rebecca. Write ✔ or ✘ in the boxes.

Rebecca / Alice

①
New York ✔

②
family ☐

③
☐

④
☐

⑤
☐

⑥
☐

⑦
☐

9 Write

Write sentences about Manuel.

Manuel is 15. He lives in Rio de Janeiro.

....

....

....

....

....

....

WRITING TIP

Don't always repeat names in your writing. Use pronouns. For example:

> *He*
> Manuel is 15. ~~Manuel~~ lives in Rio de Janeiro.
>
> *his*
> Manuel's sister is Sonia, and ~~Manuel's~~
> brother is ...

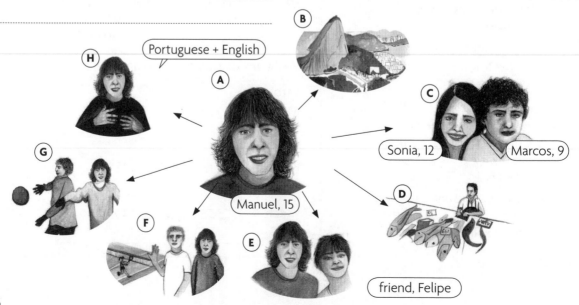

H
Portuguese + English
A
B
C
Sonia, 12   Marcos, 9
G
D
Manuel, 15
F
E
friend, Felipe

Unit check

1 Fill in the blanks

Complete the sentences with the words in the box.

| studies | doesn't | have | live | ~~her~~ | their | volleyball | don't | Tanya's | speak |

Alison Rivera and _____*her*_____ sister Tanya [1]_____ in San Diego with [2]_____ parents. The two sisters share a room. They sometimes [3]_____ fights because they [4]_____ like the same music. Tanya is in high school. Mrs. Rivera is a teacher at [5]_____ school. Tanya and Alison [6]_____ Spanish, and Tanya [7]_____ French in school. Alison [8]_____ study French. After school, they play [9]_____ together in the park.

☐ 9

2 Choose the correct answers

Ⓒircle the correct answer: a, b or c.

1 I have five brothers and _____ .

 a ⓢisters b grandmothers c fathers

2 Your mother's brother is your _____ .

 a cousin b uncle c aunt

3 Dave goes for a walk with _____ dog.

 a he b his c him

4 We have 28 people in _____ class.

 a our b their c my

5 My cousins _____ soccer.

 a like b likes c do like

6 Maria _____ in Brazil.

 a live b lives c don't live

7 _____ speak English?

 a You are b Are you c Do you

8 A: Do they work in this town?

 B: No, _____ .

 a they aren't b they do c they don't

9 Does _____ cartoons on TV?

 a she watches b you watch c Peter watch

☐ 8

3 Vocabulary

Complete the sentences with family words.

1 I have an uncle named Jim. His son is my _____*cousin*_____ Alex.

2 Karen's grandmother is Sally. Sally's husband died, so Karen doesn't have a _____ .

3 The president of the U.S. is Michelle Obama's _____, and she is the president's _____ .

4 Mrs. Smith's father is dead, so her husband doesn't have a _____ .

5 Jane and Tony love their grandparents, and their grandparents love Jane and Tony, their _____ .

6 Kate and Tom are married. Kate's brother Nick is Tom's _____ . Tom's mother is Kate's _____ , and his sister is Kate's _____ .

☐ 8

How did you do?

Total: ☐ 25

| 😊 | Very good 25 – 20 | 😐 | OK 19 – 16 | 😞 | Review Unit 5 again 15 or less |

6 Where's the market?

1 Remember and check

Complete the crossword puzzle. Check on page 36 of the Student's Book.

→ _____ ↓ _____

_____ _____

_____ _____

_____ _____

2 Vocabulary

✷ Numbers 100 +

a ▶ CD3 T24 Listen and ⊙circle⊙ the numbers you hear.

1	(139)	193
2	318	380
3	561	651
4	807	870
5	740	714
6	1,000	10,000
7	2,924	2,524

b ▶ CD3 T25 Listen and write the numbers you hear. Then write the answers in words.

1 12 + *30* = *forty-two*
2 50 + _____ = _____
3 11 + _____ = _____
4 110 + _____ = _____
5 266 + _____ = _____
6 309 + _____ = _____

3 Pronunciation

✷ /ð/ and /θ/

▶ CD3 T26 Listen to the sentences. Are the *th* sounds /θ/ (*three*) or /ð/ (*mother*)? Check (✔) the correct box. Then listen again, check and repeat.

		/θ/	/ð/
1	I <u>th</u>ink he's <u>th</u>irty.	☐	☐
2	<u>Th</u>at's <u>th</u>eir fa<u>th</u>er.	☐	☐
3	<u>Th</u>ey buy clo<u>th</u>es toge<u>th</u>er.	☐	☐
4	<u>Th</u>anks for the bir<u>th</u>day party.	☐	☐

4 Grammar

✱ *There's / there are*

a Complete the sentences with *'s* or *are*.

1 There ___'s___ a good restaurant in this town.

2 There _____ about three million people in Chicago.

3 There _____ interesting clothes in this store.

4 In New York, there _____ a river called the Hudson.

5 There _____ an expensive movie theater downtown..

6 There _____ six children in their family.

b Look at the picture and complete the text. Use *there's, there isn't, there are* or *there aren't*.

There are _____ only about 3,000 people in my town. It's very small, so [1] _____ a lot to do. [2] _____ about 12 stores downtown, and [3] _____ a good market here on Fridays, but [4] _____ any supermarkets. [5] _____ a movie theater, but that's OK. [6] _____ a great bookstore with books and some DVDs, too. [7] _____ two schools in the town and [8] _____ an excellent restaurant called the Black Horse. [9] _____ any trains here because [10] _____ a station.

5 Vocabulary

✱ *Places in towns*

a Match the words with the pictures. Write 1–8 in the boxes.

1 library
2 bank
3 train station
4 supermarket
5 newsstand
6 drugstore
7 bookstore
8 post office

Vocabulary bank Complete the sentences with the words from the box.

> elementary ~~high~~ gym shopping mall parking lot police station

1 Her children are 15 and 16. They go to _high_ school.

2 My sister is six. She goes to _____ school.

3 Where is the big _____ _____ ? We want to buy a lot of different things.

4 The _____ _____ is full. Where can we park the car?

5 There is a big _____ in my town. You can swim, practice yoga and do many other things there.

6 Look! An accident. Can you tell me where the _____ _____ is?

c Write the questions. Use *Is there a* or *Are there any*. Then write true answers.

1 good cafés / in your town?

   Are there any good cafés in your town?

   Yes, there are. or *No, there aren't.*

2 big post office / in your town?

   _____

   _____

3 bookstores / near your school?

   _____

   _____

4 good library / in your school?

   _____

   _____

5 train station / near your home?

   _____

   _____

6 newsstand / on the corner?

   _____

   _____

6 Grammar

✱ Affirmative imperatives

Write the sentences from the box under the pictures.

> Turn left.   Turn right.   Go home.
> Go straight.   Listen to me.   ~~Look!~~

1 _____   2 _____

3 _____   4 _____

5 _____   6 ___ *Look!* ___

7 Vocabulary

✱ Directions

a Look at the pictures and complete the sentences.

1 The drugstore is _next to the bookstore._

2 The park is _____ .

3 The supermarket is _____ .

   The café is _____ .

4 The bank is on _____ .

   The restaurant is _____ the _____

   and the _____ .

b Where does the tourist want to go? Look at the map and complete the dialogue. Start at the train station.

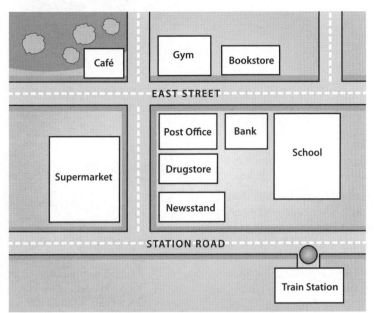

Tourist: Excuse me, where's the ¹ _____ , please?

Woman: Go down Station Road and turn right. The ² _____ is on the right between the post office and the newsstand.

Tourist: Thanks. And is there a ³ _____ near here?

Woman: Yes, there is. Turn right on East Street. The
⁴ _____ is on the left across from the bank.

Tourist: Thank you very much.

c Look at the map again. Give directions from the school to the café.

Tourist: Excuse me, is there a café near here?

You: Yes, ¹ _____ . Go ² _____ and turn
³ _____ . The café is ⁴ _____ .

8 ## Everyday English

Put the phrases in the box into the correct places.

> Wait a minute   Really   I have no idea   actually

A: See that boy? He's new in school. What's his name?

B: ¹ _____ .

A: OK. Let's go and ask him.

B: Hello. What's your name?

C: Pedro. Pedro Aguilar.

B: Pedro? Oh, you're Spanish.

C: Well, ² _____ , I'm not Spanish. I'm from Colombia.

A: ³ _____ ? That's interesting.

B: Yes, very interesting. ⁴ _____ . There's a girl in my math class. Her name's Angela. I think she's Colombian, too.

C: Yes, she is. I know her.

9 ## Study help
✱ Vocabulary

Sometimes it's a good idea to draw pictures or diagrams in your Vocabulary notebook. Draw pictures to show the meaning of these prepositions:

> ~~on~~   in   behind
> across from   between
> near   next to   under

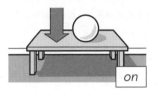

on

Skills in mind

10 Read

a Read the text and complete the table.

Paul lives in a town called Katoomba in Australia. It's in the Blue Mountains, 110 km from Sydney, and there are about 18,000 people in the town.

There isn't a museum in Katoomba, but there's a library and an excellent movie theater called The Edge. There are also a lot of stores. Paul's parents often go shopping at Coles supermarket, and they buy their newspapers at Dixon's. Paul likes bicycles, and his favorite store is Cycletech. His brother George sells books at a bookstore called Elizabeth's. Paul goes to Katoomba High School, and his little sister goes to Katoomba North Public School.

Katoomba is very popular with tourists, so there are a lot of hotels in the town. Tourists often come from Sydney by train. The trip takes two hours.

Name	Type of business/store
1 The Edge	_movie theater_
2 Coles	....
3	newsstand
4	bicycle store
5 Elizabeth's	....

b Read the text again and answer the questions. Write short answers.

1 Is Sydney very close to Katoomba?

   No, it isn't. ....

2 Are there 20,000 people in Katoomba?

   ....

3 Do people watch movies at The Edge?

   ....

4 Is there a museum in the town?

   ....

5 Do people buy clothes at Elizabeth's?

   ....

6 Is Paul's sister a student at his school?

   ....

7 Are there a lot of tourists in Katoomba?

   ....

8 Is there a train station in the town?

   ....

READING TIP

Completing a table

Exercise 10a asks you to find information in the text and put it in a table.

- First, read the text.
- Now look at the table. Read the two headings and think about the words under them.
- Read the text again and find the names of stores. They all start with a capital letter. But be careful! *Sydney*, *Blue Mountains* and *Katoomba* have capital letters, but they're names of places, not stores.

11 Write

Write a short text about a town that you like in your country or in a different country. Think about these questions.

- Is there a river / a beach?
- Is there a movie theater? Are there any cafés and restaurants? Is there a train station?
- What stores are there?
- What's your favorite place in town?

Unit check

1 Fill in the blanks

Complete the sentences with the words in the box.

| across from | there's | ~~downtown~~ | market | are | takes | newsstand | aren't | train | between |

Martin has an apartment _downtown_ , and there ¹_____ a lot of stores on his street. His apartment is ²_____ a drugstore and a ³_____ . There's a ⁴_____ station ⁵_____ the apartment, and Martin ⁶_____ the train to school. There ⁷_____ any big supermarkets, but that's no problem. ⁸_____ a very good ⁹_____ near his apartment every Saturday.   [9]

2 Choose the correct answers

(Circle) the correct answer: a, b or c.

1 Change your money at the _____ .

   a (bank) b market c university

2 You can buy magazines at a _____ .

   a library b bank c newsstand

3 100,000 = _____ .

   a a million b a thousand hundred
   c a hundred thousand

4 The post office is _____ the corner.

   a on b in c in front

5 I want to mail a _____ .

   a subway b train c letter

6 Go straight and _____ left.

   a start b turn c send

7 I think there's _____ river in this town.

   a any b a c the

8 There _____ any good clothes in this store.

   a are b aren't c isn't

9 A: Is the train station near here?   B: _____

   a I have no idea. b You're welcome. c No, there isn't.

[8]

3 Vocabulary

Find eight words for places in town in the wordsnake. (There are three other words that are not about places in towns.) Write the words on the lines below.

busstationpeopleshoppingmallparkinglotcarsdepartmentstoreelementaryschoolgymchildrenpolicestationhighschool

1 _bus station_

2 _____

3 _____

4 _____

5 _____

6 _____

7 _____

8 _____

[7]

How did you do?

Total: [24]

| 🙂 | Very good 24 – 20 | 😐 | OK 19 – 16 | 🙁 | Review Unit 6 again 15 or less |

7 They have brown eyes.

1 Remember and check

Think about Sally the chimpanzee and underline the correct words. Then check with the text on page 44 of the Student's Book.

1 Sally is *four / fourteen* years old.
2 She has *blue / brown* eyes.
3 *She has / She doesn't have* a big family.
4 She *likes / doesn't like* bananas.
5 She lives in a *park / forest*.

2 Grammar

✱ *Why ...? Because ...*

a Match the questions and answers.

1 Why do people like basketball?
2 Why isn't the library open?
3 Why do you like these shoes?
4 Why are you happy today?

a Because it's my birthday.
b Because they're fashionable.
c Because it's an exciting game.
d Because today is a holiday.

✱ *has/have*

b Complete the sentences with *has/have*.

1 You ___have___ a fantastic DVD player!
2 Mr. and Mrs. Martin _____ a house near the river.
3 Sue _____ a new bicycle.
4 I _____ a very big family.
5 We _____ an excellent computer at home.
6 This town _____ two movie theaters and a museum.
7 My brother _____ an interesting collection of stamps.
8 Chimpanzees _____ four fingers on each hand.

c Look at the table to write sentences about Jessie and her brother Tom. Use the correct form of *have*.

	Jessie	Tom
a bicycle	✗	✔
a cell phone	✔	✗
a CD player	✗	✔
brown hair	✔	✗
a big family	✗	✗
brown eyes	✔	✔
a computer	✔	✗

1 Jessie / bicycle *Jessie doesn't have a bicycle.*
2 Tom / cell phone _____
3 Jessie and Tom / big family _____
4 Tom / CD player _____
5 Jessie / brown hair _____
6 Jessie and Tom / brown eyes _____
7 Tom / computer _____
8 Jessie / computer _____

d Complete the questions. Then look at the pictures and write short answers.

1. A: _____Do_____ you _____have_____ a bicycle?
   B: _____Yes, I do._____

2. A: _____ Andy _____ a computer?
   B: _____ .

3. A: _____ you _____ a DVD player?
   B: _____ .

4. A: _____ Jane _____ big eyes?
   B: _____ .

5. A: _____ your parents _____ a car?
   B: _____ .

6. A: _____ Steve _____ a big family?
   B: _____ .

e Write four true sentences with the correct form of *have* (affirmative or negative). Choose words from box A and box B.

A	B
I My parents My sister ~~My best friend~~ My friends My English teacher My aunt	an old car brown hair a nice smile blue eyes long fingers ~~fashionable clothes~~

My best friend has fashionable clothes.

_____   _____

3 Vocabulary

★ Parts of the body

a Find 11 more parts of the body in the puzzle. Write the words under the pictures.

L	A	G	X	T	O	T	(A	R	M)
A	E	Y	E	A	L	H	H	O	O
S	R	H	A	N	D	A	T	S	U
D	X	O	Q	Y	I	F	O	O	T
V	H	A	I	R	G	A	T	M	H
L	Y	N	X	M	W	C	H	E	H
E	A	F	N	O	S	E	U	A	B
G	R	A	F	K	G	C	M	R	V
F	I	N	G	E	R	D	B	Y	A

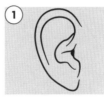
(1)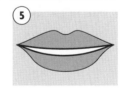
(2)
(3)

_____   _____   _____

(4)
(5)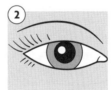
(6)

_____   _____   _____

(7)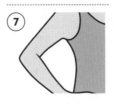
(8)
(9)

_____*arm*_____   _____   _____

(10)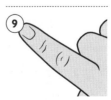
(11)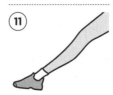
(12)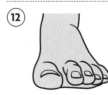

_____   _____   _____

b **Vocabulary bank** Look at the picture and write the words.

1 ....

2 ....

3 ....

4 ....

5 ....

✱ Describing people

c Complete the descriptions with the words in the box. Then draw the two people's faces.

green   nose   wavy   blond   good-looking   smile   eyes

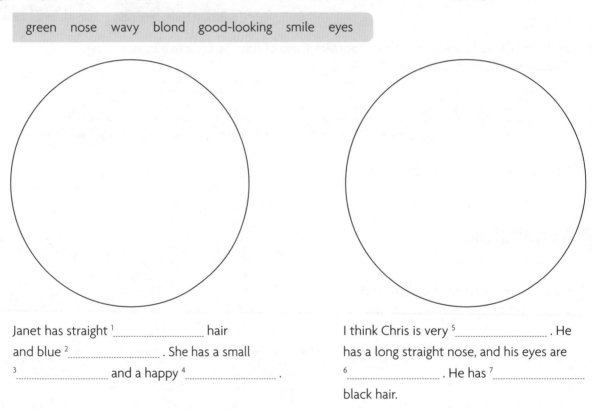

Janet has straight ¹........................ hair and blue ²........................ . She has a small ³........................ and a happy ⁴........................ .

I think Chris is very ⁵........................ . He has a long straight nose, and his eyes are ⁶........................ . He has ⁷........................ black hair.

✱ Giving personal information

d Match the questions and answers.

1 What's your last name?   a   C-L-A-R-K.

2 How do you spell that, please?   b   Yes, I do. It's 709-555-6487.

3 What's your first name?   c   I'm 15.

4 How old are you?   d   Clark.

5 What's your address?   e   538-555-1367.

6 What's your telephone number?   f   Diana.

7 Do you have a cell phone number? g   16 Felton Street, Buffalo, New York.

e ▶ **CD3 T27** Listen to the questions and reply with true information.

4 Pronunciation

✱ /v/ have

▶ **CD3 T28** Listen and repeat.

1 They have wavy hair.
2 We have 12 TVs.
3 Steve lives near the river.

4 He gives five interviews every day.
5 Vivien drives to the university.

5 Culture in mind

Look at the pictures and write the names of the animals.

bird cat cockroach ~~dog~~ fish hamster kangaroo rabbit

1 _____dog_____ 2 _____ 3 _____ 4 _____

5 _____ 6 _____ 7 _____ 8 _____

6 Study help

✱ Vocabulary

a In your Vocabulary notebook, write adjectives with their opposites. For example:

big small   awful wonderful

b Find opposites in the box and write them together in the lists.

interesting ~~long~~ cheap tall curly brown
boring straight short blond expensive ~~short~~

Adjectives for hair		Other adjectives	
_____long_____	_____short_____	_____	_____
_____	_____	_____	_____
_____	_____	_____	_____

7 Listen

▶ **CD3 T29** Joe is talking about his sister's friend. Listen and write the information in the table.

1	First name:	*Isaac*
2	Nationality:	
3	City:	*Quebec*
4	First language:	
5	Age:	
6	Color of eyes:	
7	Color of hair:	

LISTENING TIP

Listen to the spelling of *Isaac* on the recording. The speaker says "double A," like this:

I   S   double A   C.

8 Read

a Read the letter. Which picture shows David and his family?

Dear Pedro,

I'm David Ling, and I'm your new pen pal. I'm 15 and I live in Vancouver, a city in Canada. I have short black hair and brown eyes.

My mother and father are from Hong Kong, and we speak English and Chinese at home. My father works in a bank downtown, and my mother works in a restaurant. My sister doesn't live at home, because she has a job in a library in San Francisco. She's 22. My brother Jack goes to college in Vancouver, and he studies computer science.

Please write and tell me about you and your family.

All the best,

David

①

②

③

b Correct these sentences.

1 David's 14. *No, he isn't. He's 15.*

2 He has long hair.

3 His parents are from Canada.

4 His mother doesn't have a job.

5 His sister lives in a library.

6 Jack works in a computer store.

Unit check

1 Fill in the blanks

Complete the sentences with the words in the box.

| clothes   eyes   brown   ~~are~~   wears   he   isn't   don't   good-looking   wavy |

Paul and Harry _____are_____ my brothers. Harry looks like my dad. He ¹_____ very tall, and
²_____ has blond ³_____ hair. He wears fashionable ⁴_____ , and he thinks
he's very ⁵_____ . Paul and I are also pretty short, but we ⁶_____ have blond hair.
Our hair is ⁷_____ . We have green ⁸_____ , and Paul ⁹_____ glasses. [9]

2 Choose the correct answers

(Circle) the correct answer: a, b or c.

1 You have long arms and _____ .

   a foot   b mouths   c (legs)

2 Julie's eyes are _____ .

   a brown   b blond   c pink

3 I think your brother's very _____ .

   a curly   b wavy   c good-looking

4 She has short _____ hair.

   a long   b straight   c medium-length

5 Rabbits have big _____ .

   a nose   b ears   c faces

6 My first name is Helen, and my _____ is Johnson.

   a last name   b age   c address

7 A lot of people _____ pets at home.

   a are   b have   c has

8 A: Does Denise have a cell phone?

   B: Yes, she _____ .

   a have   b has   c does

9 Alan _____ glasses.

   a don't have   b doesn't has   c doesn't have [8]

3 Vocabulary

Write the letters in the correct order to make words.

1 eken   _____knee_____

2 twsri   _____

3 keche   _____

4 psli   _____

5 ealnk   _____

6 kcen   _____

7 wbleo   _____

8 weebyor   _____

9 kbca   _____ [8]

How did you do?

Total: [25]

| 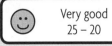 Very good 25 – 20 | OK 19 – 16 | Review Unit 7 again 15 or less |

8 This is delicious!

1 Remember and check

Match the two parts of the words.
Then write the words under the
pictures.

1 grass   fly
2 su   na
3 dragon   shi
4 alli   et
5 crick   hopper
6 igua   gator

 A

 B

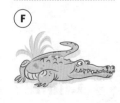 C

 D

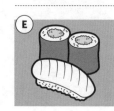 E

CHIRP

 F

2 Vocabulary

✱ Food

a ▶ CD3 T30 Listen and write the numbers 1–14.

 A

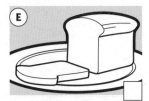 B

 C *7*

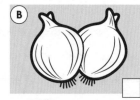 D

 E

 F

 G

 H

 I S

 J

 K

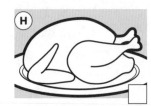 L

 M

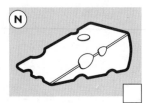 N

b Where can you find these foods in the supermarket? Write the foods
in the table.

Meat and milk	Fresh fruits and vegetables		Other groceries
yogurt			

c **Vocabulary bank** Underline the word that is different from the others.

1 salt   pepper   <u>chocolate</u>
2 chocolate   ice cream   cereal
3 beans   mushrooms   steak

4 banana   yogurt   apple
5 onion   cheese   garlic

3 Grammar

✱ Count and noncount nouns

a Write the words in the correct lists.

> ~~banana~~ ~~rice~~ onion carrot cheese
> salt apple sugar

Count	Noncount
banana	_rice_
....	....
....	....
....	....

b Look at these word pairs. Which word is count and which is noncount?
Write C or NC.

1 fruit   _NC_   orange   _C_
2 sandwich   ....   bread   ....
3 beef   ....   burger   ....
4 yogurt   ....   café   ....
5 market   ....   food   ....
6 lettuce   ....   tomato   ....
7 dessert   ....   cherry   ....

c Complete the sentences with *a*, *an* or *some*.

1 I want to buy _some_ fruit at the market.
2 Let's go shopping and get .... food.
3 I'd like .... orange, please.
4 I have .... sandwich and .... fruit.
5 We need .... rice and .... onions.
6 It isn't .... newsstand. It's .... bookstore.
7 He wants .... cheese and .... apple.

d Write the words under the pictures with *a*, *an* or *some*.

1 _some lettuce_   2 ....

3 ....   4 ....

5 ....   6 ....

7 ....   8 ....

✱ this/that/these/those

e Complete the sentences with *this*, *that*, *these* or *those*.

1 There are some great CDs in
_____*that*_____ store.

2 Mom! Look at _____ snails!

3 _____ apple's very good!

4 Wow! _____ players are
good!

5 _____ book's expensive.

6 **Boy:** What's _____ ?
Dad: It's a kangaroo.

✱ I'd like ... / Would you like ... ?

f <u>Underline</u> the correct words in the dialogue.

Woman: Good morning. ¹<u>*Can I help you?*</u> / *Would you like?*

Man: Yes, ²*I like / I'd like* three kilos of potatoes, please.

Woman: OK. ³*Do you like / Would you like* anything else?

Man: Yes, ⁴*I'd like / you'd like* some bananas – a kilo, please.

Woman: Fine. That's $6.25, please. ⁵*Do you like / Would you like* a bag?

Man: Yes, please.

g Jane is in a restaurant. Put the waiter's words in order to make questions, and then write Jane's answers.

Waiter: to / ready / you / Are / order

1 *Are you ready to order?*

Jane: (yes / roast chicken)

2 _____

Waiter: soup / like / or / you / salad / Would

3 _____

Jane: (soup)

4 _____

Waiter: drink / like / would / to / What / you

5 _____

Jane: (water)

6 _____

Waiter: like / you / else / Would / anything

7 _____

Jane: (no)

8 _____

4 Pronunciation

✳ /w/ *would*

a ▶ **CD3 T31** Listen and repeat.

1 The Swiss waiter has wavy hair.
2 We want some white rice.
3 William has a wonderful dishwasher.
4 Would you like some water with your sandwich?

b ▶ **CD3 T32** In these sentences, there are three words with a silent *w*. Underline them. Then listen, check and repeat.

1 Which answer is correct?
2 What's wrong with you?
3 Who's the winner?
4 Where does Wendy write letters?

6 Study help

✳ Grammar and vocabulary

a Put count and noncount nouns together in lists, for example:

a/an   *banana*   some   *cheese*
       egg   *rice*

b Add these words to the two lists.

> potato   water   meat   cherry   mayonnaise
> mushroom

c In your Vocabulary notebook, make two lists like the ones in Exercise 6a. Write all the words you know for food and drinks in the lists.

d A good dictionary gives symbols for count and noncount* nouns. Look at these examples.

> **garlic** /ˈɡɑrlɪk/ *noun* [U] a vegetable like a small onion
> **cookie** /ˈkʊki/ *noun* [C] a thin flat cake that is sweet

*Noncount nouns are also called uncountable nouns.

5 Everyday English

Complete the dialogues. Use one word from Box A and Box B each time.

A	B
Yes,	right.
No,	worry.
Oh,	please.
Don't	thanks.

1 A: Hitomi knows a lot about Japan. She's from Tokyo.

   B: .... Let's go and talk to her!

2 A: Do you want an apple?

   B: .... I'm hungry, and I love apples!

3 A: This math problem is very difficult! I can't do it.

   B: .... , Steve. I can help you.

4 A: Let's watch the baseball game on television.

   B: Baseball? .... I don't like baseball at all!

7 Listen

a ▶ **CD3 T33** Listen to a conversation between Martin and his mother. What food do they have at home and what don't they have? Write ✔ or ✗.

1 chicken   ✔
2 beef   ☐
3 cheese   ☐
4 tomatoes   ☐
5 apples   ☐
6 mayonnaise ☐

b What sandwich does Martin decide to have?

WRITING TIP

Writing lists

Look at how you write lists of words.

I like apples, oranges and grapes.

I want some eggs, some onions, some lettuce and some cheese.

Notice the commas (,) and the use of *and* before the last thing in the list.

8 Write

a Martin and Harry are having a party at Harry's house on Saturday. Read Martin's email about food at the party.

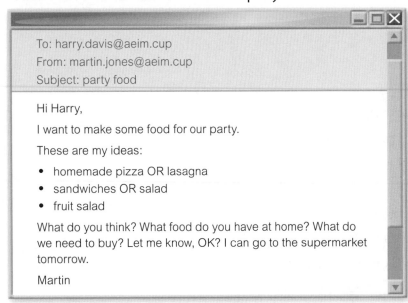

To: harry.davis@aeim.cup
From: martin.jones@aeim.cup
Subject: party food

Hi Harry,

I want to make some food for our party.

These are my ideas:

- homemade pizza OR lasagna
- sandwiches OR salad
- fruit salad

What do you think? What food do you have at home? What do we need to buy? Let me know, OK? I can go to the supermarket tomorrow.

Martin

b Imagine you are Harry. Write an email in reply to Martin and answer his questions about food.

Hi Martin,

I like your ideas for party food. Let's have ...

At home I have ...

I also have ...

I want you to buy ...

Unit check

1 Fill in the blanks

Complete the sentences with the words in the box.

> vegetables ~~beef~~ dessert sandwich meat fruit an some meal eat

We always have roast _____beef_____ or lamb for lunch on Sunday. It's my favorite [1]_____. We eat the [2]_____ with potatoes and other [3]_____ , and then we have some [4]_____ or ice cream for [5]_____ . On school days, I don't [6]_____ a big lunch. I make a [7]_____ in the morning, and I eat it at lunchtime with [8]_____ orange or [9]_____ grapes.

9

2 Choose the correct answers

(Circle) the correct answer: a, b or c.

1 A: I need some food!

   B: _____

   a What's wrong?   b (Have a sandwich.)   c Do you think so?

2 Are you _____ to order?

   a ready   b delicious   c raw

3 A: Do you have any vegetables?

   B: Yes, we have some mushrooms and some _____ .

   a oranges   b onions   c grapes

4 Does Tom want _____ apple?

   a a   b an   c some

5 I want some _____ for the salad.

   a salt   b mushroom   c lettuce

6 A: _____ you like some cheese?

   B: Yes, please.

   a Would   b Do   c Have

7 I'd like some _____ , please.

   a rice   b strawberry   c tomato

8 Do you know _____ woman in the white car?

   a this   b that   c these

9 These tomatoes are OK, but _____ bananas don't look fresh.

   a this   b that   c those

8

3 Vocabulary

(Circle) the correct word in each sentence.

1 Vegetarians don't eat (meat) / carrots.
2 Don't put a lot of cereal / salt in the soup. It's not good for you.
3 Is there too much garlic / coffee in the spaghetti?
4 For breakfast, I often have olive oil / yogurt with some fruit in it.
5 Most people put salt and sugar / pepper on their eggs.
6 To make a sandwich, you need bread / rice.
7 We need some cheese / strawberries for the pizza.
8 For dessert, you can have fruit or steak / ice cream.
9 In some countries, people eat insects: for example, fried potatoes / grasshoppers.

8

How did you do?

Total: **25**

| 😊 | Very good 25 – 20 | 😐 | OK 19 – 16 | 😞 | Review Unit 8 again 15 or less |

9 I sometimes watch TV.

1 Remember and check

Think back to the text about Caleb and Mawar. <u>Underline</u> the correct words. Then check with the text on page 58 of the Student's Book.

1   Caleb and Mawar both live *far away from a big city* / *in a big city*.

2   Caleb lives *on an island* / *in a village*.

3   He goes to school *on foot* / *by boat*.

4   His mother *is a teacher* / *works in a hotel*.

5   Mawar's home is in *Maine* / *West Java*.

6   She goes to school with *seven other children* / *a hundred other children*.

7   She *likes* / *doesn't like* the school in her village.

8   Mawar's family *has* / *doesn't have* a computer in their home.

2 Vocabulary

✳ The days of the week

a Put the days of the week in the correct order.

> ednwdsaye   yundas   iyfard   ustdeay   trusaayd   ~~ondmya~~   ytuhrsad

Weekdays: ___Monday___ _____ _____ _____ _____

Weekend: _____ _____

b Match the days to the activities. Then answer the questions about Karen's week.

Mon   Tues   Wed   Thurs   Fri   Sat   Sun

1   When does Karen go shopping?
   On Fridays.

2   When does Karen watch her favorite TV show?
   _____

3   When does she play volleyball?
   _____

4   When does she see her grandmother?
   _____

5   When does she have a piano lesson?
   _____

6   When does she study at the library?
   _____

7   When does she go to the movies?
   _____

c Write four sentences about things you do on different days.

1   _____

2   _____

3   _____

4   _____

3 Grammar

✱ Adverbs of frequency

a Put the adverbs in the correct order.

~~never~~ always often hardly ever usually sometimes

100% ── 0%

1 _____ 2 _____ 3 _____ 4 _____ 5 _____ 6 _never_

b Put the adverbs in the correct place in the sentence.

1 Susan wears black shoes. (usually)

Susan usually wears black shoes.

2 Robert plays ice hockey with his friends. (often)

....

3 Tony and Philip are on the school bus. (never)

....

4 Beth listens to classical music. (hardly ever)

....

5 We have pizza on Fridays. (always)

....

6 The music on this radio station is fantastic. (usually)

....

7 My parents help me with my homework. (sometimes)

....

c How often do you do these things? Write true sentences. Use adverbs from Exercise 3a.

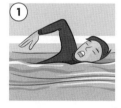    

| go swimming on Sundays | have a burger at lunchtime | go to bed before ten o'clock | listen to the radio in bed | watch TV before school |

1 _I sometimes go swimming on Sundays._

2 ....

3 ....

4 ....

5 ....

d Look at the information about Alex. Write sentences about him.

	Mon	Tues	Wed	Thur	Fri	Sat	Sun
have an English class		✔		✔		✔	
play baseball						✔	✔
write letters							✔
walk to school	✔	✔	✔	✔	✔		

1 _Alex has an English class three times a week._

2 He ....

3 ....

4 ....

e Write sentences with frequency expressions (for example, *twice a day, every morning*).

Matthew

Julie

Danny

Denise

Greg

1 *Matthew takes the train twice a day.*

2 ....

3 ....

4 ....

5 ....

4 Vocabulary

✱ TV shows

a (Circle) seven more kinds of TV shows in the wordsnake.

newssoapoperatalkshowsitcomcartoongameshowdocumentaryrealityshow

b Read about some of the shows on TV tonight. Write the types of shows.

1 Tonight, David Letterman talks to two great movie stars. _____*talk show*_____

2 We have soccer from Mexico and skiing from Colorado. _____

3 The latest information from around the world on *World News Tonight*. _____

4 Tonight: *The Simpsons*. _____

5 On tonight's show, Mary sees Bill going out with Amanda, and she isn't happy about it!

_____

6 Lots of laughs and smiles with the popular Ray Romano. _____

7 The prize tonight: $25,000!! _____

8 This week: Life in Japan. _____

5 Pronunciation

✱ Compound nouns

a ▶ **CD3 T34** Add the words in the box to make new nouns. Listen and check.

> work   berry   paper   friend
> day   fly   ~~fast~~   time

1 break *fast*_____   5 straw_____

2 week_____   6 news_____

3 lunch_____   7 dragon_____

4 home_____   8 girl_____

b ▶ **CD3 T34** Where is the stress in each word? Listen again and repeat.

6 Vocabulary

⭐ What time is it?

a Look at the pictures and write the times in list 1–6. Then match them with the other expressions in list a–f.

1 *It's seven thirty.*   a It's twenty-five to eight.

2 It's _____   b It's seven thirty.

3 _____   c It's ten after seven.

4 _____   d It's quarter to eight.

5 _____   e It's ten to seven.

6 _____   f It's quarter after six.

b ▶ **CD3 T35** Listen and write the times in number form. Then listen again and check your answers.

1 _*11:55*_   2 _____   3 _____   4 _____   5 _____   6 _____

7 Culture in mind

Complete the summary about Carmen. Use the words in the box. Then check with the text on page 62 of the Student's Book.

never   also   always   lives   hardly ever   every day   sometimes

Carmen is 16, and she ¹ _____ in San Francisco. She doesn't watch television ² _____ because she thinks it can be a waste of time. But she ³ _____ watches *America's Got Talent.* It's her favorite show. She likes learning about other countries, so she ⁴ _____ watches documentaries.

On weekends, she ⁵ _____ watches cartoons. She ⁶ _____ watches sports programs. She doesn't like them at all. And she ⁷ _____ watches the news.

8 Study help

⭐ Grammar

a Learn the parts of speech. Look at the sentence. What parts of speech are the <u>underlined</u> words?

Sam <u>often</u> <u>wears</u> <u>white</u> <u>shoes</u>.

Nouns	Verbs	Adjectives	Adverbs
shoes	*wears*	*white*	*often*
_____	_____	_____	_____
_____	_____	_____	_____
_____	_____	_____	_____

b Add the words in the box to the lists. If you aren't sure about a word, try using it in a sentence.

black   never   buys   sandwiches   sometimes coffee   always   delicious   has   expensive clothes   makes

c Make new sentences with the four parts of speech. There are many possible answers!

Sam ____*never buys expensive clothes.*____

_____

Jill _____

_____

Jack _____

_____

Rosa _____

_____

9 Read

a Read the text and choose the best title.

1 Television in an American home
2 Soap operas on American TV
3 Sports programs on TV in the U.S.

TELEVISION is very important in many American homes. On average, American families watch about 150 hours of television a month. The nation's favorite shows are dramas like *Lost*, a show about a group of people lost on an island. Sitcoms, game shows and reality TV shows are also popular.

We talked to one family, the Moores from Dallas, Texas, about how they watch TV. Mr. Steve Moore (42) isn't typical. He doesn't watch a lot of TV, but he usually watches the news. He sometimes watches sports like baseball or golf on weekends.

The two children love TV. Jimmy (12) watches every day, usually for about three hours. His favorite shows are sitcoms and some cartoon shows like *The Simpsons*. His sister, Rita (16), watches her favorite soap opera every day, when she can. "I love soaps," she says, "and reality shows like *American Idol* are good, too." Mrs. Barbara Moore (38) likes watching TV on weekends when there's a good movie on. "I love old movies," she says. "And I often watch documentaries, too."

Like many American families, the Moores have two televisions in their home, and the members of the family watch different things at different times. Do they watch anything together? "Yes," says Jimmy. "We all watch American football games when the Dallas Cowboys are playing."

READING TIP

Choosing a title for a text

In Exercise 9a, all the words in the three titles are in the text. But two of these aren't good titles because they go with only one small part of the text.

- Read the text from beginning to end before you decide about the title.
- Don't just look for words. Think about general ideas.
- Remember, the title is for the *whole* text.

b Read the text again and answer the questions.

1 How many hours of television do American families watch each month?
About 150 hours a month.

2 Does Mr. Moore watch many game shows?
---

3 Which kinds of shows does Jimmy like?
---

4 Does he watch TV seven days a week?
---

5 What is Rita's favorite kind of show?
---

6 When does Mrs. Moore watch movies?
---

7 What does the family watch together?
---

10 Listen

a ▶ CD3 T36 Listen to an interview about TV. How often does the woman watch TV?
---

b ▶ CD3 T36 Listen again and check (✔) the correct adverbs.

	never	hardly ever	usually
1 sitcoms			✔
2 documentaries			
3 soap operas			
4 the news			

Unit check

1 Fill in the blanks

Complete the sentences with the words in the box.

| on | at | every | usually | do | comes | news | ~~weekdays~~ | days | soap |

On __weekdays__ I leave school [1]_____ 3:45 in the afternoon. I [2]_____ walk home with my friend Diane, but [3]_____ Wednesdays I have a swimming lesson after school. Diane often [4]_____ over to my house, and we watch our favorite [5]_____ opera. It's on at 5:30, five [6]_____ a week. We also watch the [7]_____ at six o'clock. I [8]_____ my homework after dinner [9]_____ evening, so I don't watch a lot of TV.

[9]

2 Choose the correct answers

(Circle) the correct answer: a, b or c.

1 We can get a lot of information from
_____.

  a (documentaries) b sitcoms
  c soap operas

2 People try to win money on _____.

  a talk shows b game shows
  c sports programs

3 Quarter after four is _____.

  a 4:15 b 4:30 c 4:45

4 _____ time is it?

  a When b What c Where

5 10:40 is _____.

  a forty to ten b twenty to eleven
  c twenty after eleven

6 The day before Thursday is _____.

  a Wednesday b Friday c Monday

7 Sandra isn't at home. She _____ goes shopping on Saturday.

  a never b hardly ever c always

8 I check my email three times _____ day.

  a the b a c of the

9 _____ do you watch soap operas?

  a Which b How many c How often

[8]

3 Vocabulary

Complete the sentences with the words in the box. There are three words you do not need.

| ten after ten twenty-five to ten Wednesday ~~talk shows~~ Monday news game show sitcom Saturday cartoons documentaries reality show |

1 My sister loves __talk shows__. She thinks it's great when big stars talk about their lives.

2 My mom is on a _____ next week. I hope she wins a lot of money!

3 I always watch the _____. I want to know what's going on in the world.

4 I love _____. It's interesting to learn how people in other countries live.

5 It's ten to nine now. In 45 minutes it's
_____.

6 My favorite day is _____. I can stay up and watch the late-night talk shows because on Sundays I can sleep longer.

7 I love the weekend, and I always find it difficult to get up on _____ mornings.

8 My favorite show is called *Just for Laughs*. It's a _____, and it's very funny.

9 I don't like _____ very much. I think they are for young children.

[8]

How did you do?

Total: [25]

| 😊 | Very good 25 – 20 | 😐 | OK 19 – 16 | ☹ | Review Unit 9 again 15 or less |

10 Don't do that!

1 Remember and check

▶ CD3 T37 Can you complete the dialogue between Julie and Steve? Complete the sentences. Then listen and check.

Steve: This movie's ¹ _____awful_____ . I'm bored. Really bored.

Julie: Me, too. And I'm ² _____ . I mean, I don't understand the story. What's that?

Steve: What?

Julie: That noise. What is it?

Steve: Hmm. I don't know. Stay ³ _____ .

Julie: Don't go outside! I'm ⁴ _____ .

Steve: Don't ⁵ _____ , Julie. Everything's OK.

Julie: Steve? Where are you? Come ⁶ _____ !

Julie: Help!

Steve: It's me!

Julie: Oh, Steve, you're ⁷ _____ ! Don't do that!

Steve: Sorry, Julie. It's just a joke.

Julie: Oh, Steve. You're not very ⁸ _____ .

2 Grammar

✱ Negative imperatives

a Complete the dialogues with the verbs in the box.

> be talk shout cry

1 **A:** What's the matter, Cynthia?

   B: It's awful here. I miss my friends at home.

   A: I know you're unhappy. But please don't _____ .

2 **A:** That's the new boy, Claudio. He's from Ecuador.

   B: His English isn't very good.

   A: Don't _____ about his English. You don't speak Spanish!

3 **A:** Hi, Mom! I'm home!

   B: Shhh! Don't _____ ! Your dad's asleep!

4 **A:** I want to take a picture of you in front of the museum.

   B: Oh, no! I hate pictures of myself!

   A: Don't _____ like that. Come on!

b Read the text. Complete the advice with the verbs in the box.

> Ask ~~Listen~~ Don't eat Go Listen
> Write Don't tell Talk Don't sit

Advice for teens

When you or your friends are in trouble …

We all have good and bad days. When you have a problem, here are some things you can do:

- _____Listen_____ to music and try to relax.

- ¹ _____ the problem on a piece of paper. Then make a list of things you can do and put them in order.

- ² _____ a lot of food. It doesn't make you feel better.

- ³ _____ in the house.
  ⁴ _____ for a walk. Exercise is good for you.

- ⁵ _____ to a friend about your problem.

What can you do when a friend has a problem? Here are some ideas:

- ⁶ _____ to your friend. Don't talk a lot.

- ⁷ _____ questions. Help your friend to talk openly.

- Your friend's problem is private.
  ⁸ _____ other people about it.

Write imperative sentences. Use affirmative or negative forms of the verbs in the box.

look at   ~~eat~~   go   open   turn on   talk

①

②

③

④

⑤

⑥

1   *Eat your vegetables.*

2   *Don't*

3

4

5

6

3 Pronunciation

✱ *Linking sounds*

▶ **CD3 T38**   Listen to the sentences. <u>Underline</u> the word *don't* when you hear the *t*.

1   <u>Don't</u> leave school now.

2   I don't know where she is.

3   Don't play that music. I don't like it.

4   Please don't ask a lot of questions.

5   I don't understand why he's so angry.

6   Don't eat all the chocolate!

7   Don't open the box.

8   I don't think it's a good idea.

4 Vocabulary

★ How do you feel?

a In the puzzle, find seven more words to describe feelings. Write the words under the pictures (1–8).

A	E	X	C	I	T	E	D	W	W
A	R	W	O	R	R	I	E	D	O
S	R	U	N	S	A	D	P	J	R
C	F	F	F	H	H	A	I	S	B
A	G	I	U	A	F	N	P	A	O
R	N	Z	S	P	J	G	L	H	R
E	E	T	E	P	N	R	Q	A	E
D	X	C	D	Y	G	Y	W	P	D

1 _____

2 _____

3 _____

4 _____ *excited* _____

b <u>Underline</u> the correct words.

1 Look! There's a snake! I'm *angry /* <u>*scared*</u>.

2 This show's awful. We're *bored / scared*.

3 Our teacher smiles a lot. She's always *happy / unhappy*.

4 I don't know what to do. I'm *happy / confused*.

5 It's my little sister's birthday tomorrow. She's really *excited / angry*.

6 My father has a problem. He's *worried / happy*.

7 Lee doesn't have any friends here. He's *excited / unhappy*.

8 I don't have my homework with me. The teacher's *angry / confused*.

5 _____

6 _____

7 _____

8 _____

c ▶ **CD3 T39** Listen to the five speakers. Match them with the feelings and the reasons they feel this way. Then write sentences.

Speaker	Feeling	Why?
1	confused	There's a problem with the computer.
2	worried	She's the winner of a trip to Paris.
3	bored	It's late, and her daughter isn't home.
4	angry	He doesn't have anything to do.
5	excited	The homework is difficult.

1 *Speaker 1 is bored because he doesn't have anything to do.*

2 *Speaker 2* _____

3 _____

4 _____

5 _____

d Look at these examples.

We're interested in these books. (describes a person's feeling)

These books are interesting. (describes something that produces a feeling)

Complete the dialogues. Choose adjectives from the box.

> confused confusing excited exciting
> worried worrying bored boring

1 A: This show's _____ .
   B: I think so, too. Let's turn off the TV.

2 A: My grandmother is in the hospital.
   B: Oh, no! Really?
   A: Yes, we're all very
      _____ about her.

3 A: What's the answer to question 3? I don't understand it.
   B: I have no idea. I think the question's very _____ .

4 A: Why is the dog so
      _____ ?
   B: Because she knows Leo's coming. He always takes her for a walk in the afternoon.

e **Vocabulary bank** Write the letters in the correct order to make words.

1 There's an important test this morning, so I'm feeling very <u>dsetrsse</u>   *stressed*   .

2 I'm not worried about the test! I'm very <u>deerlax</u> _____ about it!

3 It's very late, and I'm feeling <u>eplyse</u> _____ . I think it's time to go to bed!

4 I can't find my cat! I'm very <u>stpeu</u> _____ about it.

5 I feel <u>ercefluh</u> _____ today. It's a holiday!

6 Don't be <u>itedfngher</u> _____ ! This dog is very friendly!

5 Everyday English

Underline the correct words.

1 A: Do you like spaghetti Bolognese?
   B: Yes, *the thing is / I think* it's delicious.

2 A: *What's wrong / The thing is*, Alex?
   B: I'm very tired. Really tired!

3 A: Let's listen to this CD.
   B: No, thanks. It's late, and *anyway / I think*, I don't like that CD.

4 A: Let's go to the movies tonight.
   B: No, thanks.
   A: Why not?
   B: Well, *I think / the thing is*, I don't have any money.

6 Study help

✳ Vocabulary

In your Vocabulary notebook write examples to help you learn how to use new words. For example:

excited (I feel <u>excited</u> before a big party.)
bored (I feel <u>bored</u> when I watch golf on TV.)

Think of your own example sentences for these adjectives.

excited (_____
_____)

scared (_____
_____)

bored (_____
_____)

worried (_____
_____)

happy (_____
_____)

7 Read

Read Jennifer's letter to a magazine and write *T* (true) or *F* (false).

Clara's PROBLEM PAGE

Dear Clara,

I'm 14, and I'm really unhappy. Please help me!

My mom, my brother and I have moved from New York City to San Diego, California. My mom is a computer programmer, and she has a new job at a college here. We live in a new house, and I go to a new school. It's a nice place, but everything is new for me! New teachers, new students in my class, new school work! I really miss my old friends from New York. I even miss my teachers there! And I'm worried about my school work. Sometimes I'm confused because it's different from the work at my old school.

I feel very alone, but what can I do? Please don't tell me to talk to my mom. She works eight hours a day, and she's always tired. She never has time for me. And my brother? He's only 10, so he can't help me.

San Diego is a nice city, but there are so many things I miss! Please tell me what to do.

Yours,

Jennifer

8 Write

Imagine you are Clara. Write an answer to Jennifer. Give her some advice.

Dear Jennifer,
I'm sorry you're sad, and I understand your problem. Here are some ideas. ...

WRITING TIP

Planning your writing

Before you write to Jennifer, make notes about the things you want to say to her. Organize your ideas under these headings:

General ideas	Friends	School work
	Keeping old friends	
	Making new friends	

1 Jennifer isn't happy, and she needs some help. [T]
2 She and her family live in New York City. [ ]
3 Her mother works at a computer store. [ ]
4 Jennifer doesn't miss her old friends. [ ]
5 She has problems with her studies at school. [ ]
6 Jennifer's mother doesn't talk to her about her problems. [ ]
7 Jennifer often talks to her brother. [ ]

Unit check

1 Fill in the blanks

Complete the dialogue with the words in the box.

| matter listen ~~you~~ help angry happy worried don't fine boyfriend |

Rosa: Are _____you_____ OK, Lynn? You don't look very ¹ _____ .

Lynn: Oh, I'm ² _____ .

Rosa: Come on. What's the ³ _____ ?

Lynn: Oh, I'm ⁴ _____ with Janet Martin. She's saying bad things about my ⁵ _____ .

Rosa: Lynn, don't ⁶ _____ to her. She isn't a very nice person.

Lynn: Yes, I guess you're right.

Rosa: Look, ⁷ _____ think about her. Come over to my house and ⁸ _____ me
with my English. I'm ⁹ _____ about the test tomorrow.

Lynn: OK, let's go.

9

2 Choose the correct answers

(Circle) the correct answer: a, b or c.

1 I think this music is _____ .

  a (boring) b bored c worried

2 Is this word right or wrong? I'm _____ .

  a confused b excited c scared

3 Tom's _____ because his pet hamster is
dead.

  a angry b worried c sad

4 Turn _____ the television, please.

  a in b on c out

5 Laura's a happy person. She smiles and _____
a lot.

  a shouts b cries c laughs

6 Go _____ ! I'm trying to listen to the radio.

  a over b away c straight on

7 Please don't go! _____ here!

  a Is b Back c Stay

8 Please leave me _____ .

  a alone b around c about

9 I don't want to talk to you. _____ me again.

  a Call b Phone c Don't call   8

How did you do?

Total: [ ] 25

3 Vocabulary

In each sentence, <u>underline</u> the word
that does <u>not</u> fit.

1 My friend Alex smiles a lot. He's very
happy / relaxed / <u>unhappy</u>.

2 This is very bad book. I'm really *bored /
excited / confused*.

3 Mom has a problem. She's *worried /
unhappy / happy*.

4 We talk in class, and the teacher is *angry
/ scared / unhappy*.

5 I hate big dogs. I'm *frightened / scared /
bored* of them.

6 It's my birthday tomorrow. I'm *excited /
happy / sleepy*.

7 My sister's rabbit is dead. She's very
excited / upset / unhappy.

8 This test is easy! I'm really *angry /
relaxed / happy*!

9 My uncle is in the hospital. He's very sick.
I'm *upset / worried / bored*.   8

| Very good 25 – 20 |  OK 19 – 16 | 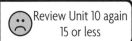 Review Unit 10 again 15 or less |

11 Yes, I can!

1 Remember and check

Complete the summary of the text about Rick Hoyt. Use the verbs in the box. Then check with the text on page 72 of the Student's Book.

| swim | uses | ride | pulls | participate | works | sits | pushes |

Rick Hoyt has cerebral palsy, but he [1]_____ at a college, and he [2]_____ a computer to communicate. Rick and his father also [3]_____ in triathlons together. Rick can't run, so his father [4]_____ him in a wheelchair. He can't [5]_____ , so his father [6]_____ him through the water in a boat. And he can't [7]_____ a bike, so he [8]_____ in a seat on the front of his father's bike.

2 Grammar

✱ can / can't (ability)

a Look at the pictures. Write a sentence for each picture.

1 _She can sing._

2 _____

3 _____

4 _____

5 _____

6 _____

b Write questions for the activities in Exercise 2a. Start with *Can you ...?* Then write true answers (*Yes, I can. / No, I can't.*).

1 _Can you sing?_

_____

2 _____

_____

3 _____

_____

_____

4 _____

_____

5 _____

_____

6 _____

_____

c Look at the information in the table and complete the sentences.

Sylvia	✔	✘	✘	✘
Paul	✔	✔	✘	✔
George	✔	✘	✔	✔
Eva	✘	✔	✘	✘

1 A: _____Can_____ George walk on his hands?

   B: _No__ , he ___can't____ .

2 Sylvia _____ stand on her head, but she _____ walk on her hands.

3 Paul and George _____ juggle.

4 Sylvia, Paul and Eva _____ ride a horse.

5 A: _____ Sylvia and Eva juggle?

   B: _____ , they _____ .

6 A: _____ Paul and Sylvia walk on their hands?

   B: Paul _____ , but Sylvia _____ .

d Make true sentences. Use your own ideas.

1 I can't _____ , but
  I can _____ .

2 I can _____ , but
  I can't _____ .

3 My parents can _____
  _____ , but they can't _____
  _____ .

4 My best friend can _____
  _____ , but he/she _____
  _____ .

5 A chimpanzee can't _____
  _____ , but it can _____
  _____ .

6 Young children can _____
  _____ , but they can't _____
  _____ .

3 Pronunciation

✱ can/can't

a ▶ CD3 T40 Listen to the questions and answers. <u>Underline</u> the words that are stressed.

1 Can you <u>read</u>?　　　　<u>Yes</u>, I <u>can</u>.
2 Can they write?　　　　Yes, they can.
3 Can she play the guitar?　　Yes, she can.

b ▶ CD3 T40 Listen again. This time, listen to the pronunciation of *can*. Is it the same in the questions and the answers?

c ▶ CD3 T41 Read these sentences. <u>Underline</u> the words that you think are stressed. Then listen, check and repeat.

1 I can dance, but I can't sing.
2 He can read, but he can't write.
3 Can she play the piano?
4 Can you do Sudoku puzzles?

4 Vocabulary

✴ Sports

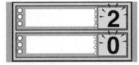
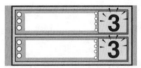

a Look at the pictures and complete the sentences.

1 John _plays volleyball_ with his friends.
2 People _____ here in the winter.
3 We _____ once a week.
4 Can James _____ ?
5 Kate _____ in the park.
6 People sometimes _____ in this river.
7 Can you _____ ?
8 We often _____ on vacation.

b Look at these lists. Complete them with more sports.

go + -ing	play + name of game
go skiing	play tennis
go riding	

c **Vocabulary bank** Underline the correct option.

1 He's a *fan* / <u>*referee*</u>.
2 The *score* / *team* is two-zero.
3 It's a *tie* / *third*.

4 My team is Brazil. They always *win* / *lose*!
5 My team is New York. They always *win* / *lose*!
6 They're very happy. They're the *fans* / *champions*!

5 Grammar

✴ *like / don't like + -ing*

a Look at the information about the people. Write sentences about them using these verbs:

	Joanna	Kevin	Brian and Louise
😀 = love			
🙂 = like			
😕 = not like			
😣 = hate			

1 *Joanna likes skiing. She loves swimming, but she doesn't like Rollerblading. She hates playing soccer.*
2 Kevin _____
_____
_____
3 Brian and Louise _____
_____
_____
_____

b Write similar sentences about you, your best friend and people in your family.

1 I _____

2 My best friend _____

3 My _____

4 My _____

6 Culture in mind

a Match the names of the sports with the pictures. Write the numbers 1–6 in the boxes.

1 track and field   2 wrestling
3 swimming   4 volleyball
5 tennis   6 gymnastics

A

B

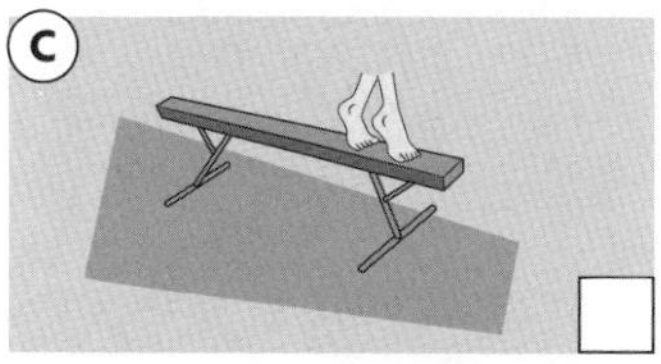

C

D

E
1

F

b Who does which sports? Write the sports from Exercise 6a under the names. Then check with the text on page 76 of the Student's Book.

Shannon   Doug

_____   _____

_____   _____

_____   _____

7 Study help

★ Pronunciation

a For help with pronunciation, group words under their sounds. For example:

/æ/	/ɔr/	/eɪ/
sad	horse	race
match	board	play

Add these words to the lists.

sports   camel   Rollerblade   take   hands   support
laugh   more   late

b Look for words in Units 10 and 11 to write under these sounds. If you aren't sure of the pronunciation, check in your dictionary.

/ɪ/	/i/	/ɑ/	/oʊ/
swim	team	hop	open
finish	wheelchair	problem	photo

8 Listen

▶ CD3 T42 Listen and choose the correct picture.
Circle A, B or C.

1 What sports does Tom do?

A   B   C

2 What can Cristina do?

A   B   C

3 What does Matt do in the winter?

A   B   C

4 What can Pete do?

A   B   C

9 Listen and write

a **▶ CD3 T43** Listen to an interview with Mark Cavalcanti. Complete the information in the box.

b Use the information in the box to write a paragraph about Mark.

Name: *Mark Cavalcanti*

Age: ¹...

Language(s): ²...

Nationality: ³...

His favorite sport: ⁴...

His other sports:

⁵...

⁶...

People in his family:

His mother...

Anna ⁷(...)

Sports they like:

His mother doesn't ⁸........................... .

Anna: ⁹........................... .

Unit check

1 Fill in the blanks

Complete the sentences with the words in the box.

| team   can   swim   doesn't   loves   races   ~~sports~~   free   guitar   volleyball |

Jackie is very good at _____*sports*_____ . She can play [1]_____ , and she's on the basketball [2]_____ at school. She can also [3]_____ well, and she often wins [4]_____ . Her brother Tim does different things in his [5]_____ time. He [6]_____ juggle and walk on his hands, and he [7]_____ playing the [8]_____ , but he [9]_____ like sports.

9

2 Choose the correct answers

Circle the correct answer: a, b or c.

1 I _____ mushrooms. I think they're awful.

  a like   b love   c (hate)

2 _____ is my favorite sport.

  a Baseball   b Singing   c Juggling

3 We often go _____ in winter.

  a snowboard   b skiing   c football

4 John _____ gymnastics twice a week after school.

  a goes   b plays   c does

5 They want to take part _____ the triathlon.

  a with   b for   c in

6 I _____ swim, but not very well.

  a can   b can't   c like

7 Barbara doesn't like team games, but she likes _____ .

  a Rollerblading   b basketball   c volleyball

8 Can you _____ a bike?

  a ride   b run   c go

9 She _____ like wrestling.

  a don't   b doesn't   c isn't

8

3 Vocabulary

Complete each sentence with a word from the box. There are two words you don't need.

| come   cycling   do   tie   go   play   ride   score   baseball   swimming   ~~volleyball~~ |

1 Let's go to the beach and play ___*volleyball*___ .
2 In the winter, we _____ skiing in the mountains. It's great!
3 In the summer, we go _____ in the river near our house.
4 It's a nice day. I want to _____ tennis with Julie.
5 It's a very exciting game. The _____ is 5–3!
6 There are nine players on a _____ team.
7 The score is 2–2. It's a _____ .
8 I'm a very good runner. I always _____ in first in races at school.
9 I really love _____ , but my bike isn't very good.

8

How did you do?

Total: 25

| ☺ Very good 25 – 20 | ☺ OK 19 – 16 | ☹ Review Unit 11 again 15 or less |

12 A bad storm's coming.

1 Remember and check

Circle the correct word. Then check on page 78 of the Student's Book.

1 John White is a *taxi* / *bus* driver.

2 John goes sailing *once* / *twice* a year with his wife and son.

3 This year John is sailing around *Australia* / *the world*.

4 Pauline calls John. He is near *South Africa* / *South America*.

5 John can see *whales* / *dolphins* next to his boat.

6 John stops talking because *a storm is coming* / *he's having breakfast*.

2 Grammar

✱ Present continuous

a Write the verbs in the *-ing* form and put them in the lists. Think about the spelling.

> ~~come~~ ~~sit~~ ~~watch~~ play
> swim write shop do
> use read take run

+ ing

.... *watching* ....

....

....

....

e + ing

.... *coming* ....

....

....

....

double letter + ing

.... *sitting* ....

....

....

....

b Complete the dialogues. Use the present continuous form of six more verbs from Exercise 2a.

1 **Max:** Where's James?

   Peggy: He's in his room. *He's reading* a book.

2 **Norma:** Is Barbara at home?

   Cynthia: No, sorry. _____ at the supermarket.

3 **Chris:** Where are Mom and Dad?

   Peter: They're in the living room. _____ a DVD.

4 **Caroline:** Do you want to go for a walk?

   Richard: No, not right now. _____ some postcards.

5 **Monica:** I can't see Nick and Petra.

   Phil: They're over there. _____ on that seat under the tree.

6 **Dad:** Tony and Frank, where are you?

   Tony: We're up here. _____ our homework.

7 **Dad:** Is Mom home?

   Kate: Yes, she's in the bathroom. _____ a shower.

c Look at the picture. Correct these false statements.

1 Anne and Peter are playing cards.

Peter isn't playing cards. He's reading.

2 George and Alice are watching TV.

3 Dorothy is talking to George.

4 Maria and Bill are listening to music.

5 Pat is dancing.

6 Martin and Wendy are playing the guitar.

d Make present continuous questions.
Then write the short answers.

1 Mom and Dad / sit in the kitchen?

Are Mom and Dad sitting in the kitchen?

✔ *Yes, they are.*

2 you / watch the news?

✗

3 Helen / do her homework?

✔

4 Ken and Neil / play tennis?

✗

5 Joe / use the computer?

✗

e Write true answers. Use the present
continuous.

1 Where are you sitting right now?

2 What are you doing?

3 What are you using?

4 Are you sitting alone in the room?

5 Are you wearing glasses?

6 What are other people doing?

✱ Present continuous and simple present

f Look at these examples. Then <u>underline</u> the correct words in the sentences.

*Janet often **goes** to the market on Saturday, but this morning she's **playing** basketball.*

*I'm **having** pizza for lunch today, but I usually **have** sandwiches.*

1 My sister *talks / <u>is talking</u>* to Sophie on the phone. *<u>They sometimes talk</u> / They're sometimes talking* for over an hour!

2 *I read / I'm reading* a lot. At the moment *I read / I'm reading* a book about Russia.

3 A: Are Philip and Greg at home?
   B: No, *they play / they're playing* tennis. *They play / They're playing* three times a week.

4 A: Where's Eva?
   B: *She visits / She's visiting* her aunt and uncle. *She often stays / She's often staying* with them for the weekend.

5 A: How does your brother get to work?
   B: *He takes / He's taking* a train. But he *doesn't work / isn't working* this week. He's on vacation.

3 Pronunciation

✱ /h/ have

▶ **CD3 T44** Listen and repeat.

1 Harry's hobby is horseback riding.
2 I'm hardly ever hungry at home.
3 He's unhappy about his hair.
4 How often does Helen help you?
5 Hannah's having a hamburger at the Hilton Hotel.

4 Vocabulary

✱ House and furniture

a Complete the crossword.

Across

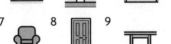

Down

b Write the parts of the house.

1 My family watches TV in this room. _____
2 We wash and take showers in this room. _____
3 We put the car here. _____
4 There's a stove and a fridge in this room. _____
5 We use these to go up to the bedrooms. _____

c **Vocabulary bank** Match the words and pictures.

1 a chest of drawers
2 a hanger
3 a shelf
4 a lamp
5 curtains
6 a mirror
7 a blanket
8 a pillow

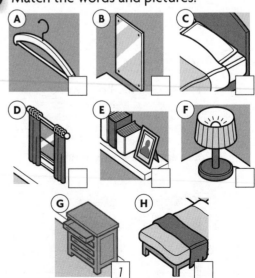

70 UNIT 12

✳ Prepositions

d ▶ **CD3 T45** Listen and complete the text with the prepositions. Then draw the missing things in the picture of the room (table, window, computer, pictures, door).

on ~~in~~ near between next to under

I have a bed and a desk _in_ my room.
There's a small table ¹_____ the
bed. The desk is ²_____ the
window, and I have my computer
³_____ the desk. There's a small
armchair in the corner of the room. On
the wall ⁴_____ the desk and
the armchair, I have three pictures of my
favorite pop stars. The door is
⁵_____ the armchair.

5 Everyday English

Complete the dialogues. Use one word from Box A and Box B each time.

A	B
Why don't	of
all	you
a little bit	right
a lot	of

1 A: The school volleyball team isn't very good. What do you think?

   B: Actually, I think there are _____ great players on the team.

2 A: Please, please help me with this homework! Please!

   B: Oh, _____! Give me the book. What's the problem?

3 A: I'm hungry. Can I have some ice cream?

   B: _____ eat an apple or a banana? They're good for you.

4 A: Would you like some soup, and then some chicken?

   B: No soup, thanks, but I'd like _____ chicken please, not a lot.

6 Study help

✳ Vocabulary

A good way to remember words is to draw a word web. Complete this word web.

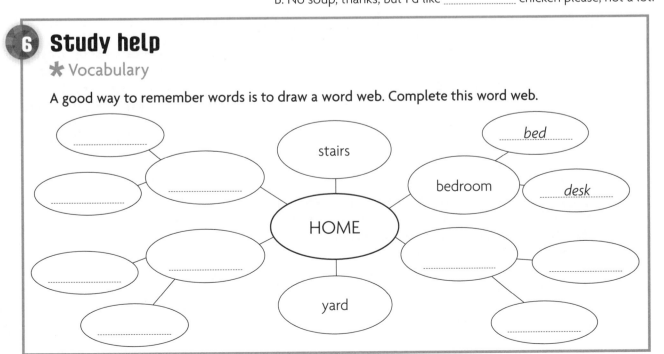

7 Read and listen

a Kate is on a school trip in Mexico. Read her postcard to her parents. In the table, write ✔ (good) or ✘ (not good) under Kate.

MEXICO
Guadalajara •
• Oaxaca

April 25th

Dear Mom and Dad,

I'm writing this from the city of Oaxaca in Mexico. The city's beautiful, but it's raining at the moment. We're staying in a small hotel. The rooms aren't very nice. They're too small and dark. I'm not doing very well with my Spanish, but I'm trying. The food's delicious. We're all having a good time.

Lots of love,

Kate

Mr. and Mrs. J. R. Thomas
32 Harbor Street
New York, NY 10012
U.S.A.

		Kate (Oaxaca)	Pam (Guadalajara)
1	Hotel	....	✔
2	Speaking the language	....	....
3	Food	....	....
4	Weather	....	....
5	Having a good time?	....	....

b ▶ CD3 T46 Pam is also on the school trip. It's three days later, and they're in Guadalajara. Listen to Pam talking to her father. In the table, write ✔ (good) or ✘ (not good) under *Pam*.

8 Write

Imagine you're a tourist on vacation in your town. Write a postcard to your parents or to a friend. Use the topics from the table on this page.

WRITING TIP

Writing a postcard

- Start with *Dear* _____ ,
- Here are some endings you can use.

  All the best,
  Love,
  Lots of love,
  Love from ...

Unit check

1 Fill in the blanks

Complete the sentences with the words in the box.

| in   is   aren't   are   finishing   reading   ~~sitting~~   they're   living   bedroom |

Right now, Jill's _____sitting_____ in front of the computer in her ¹_____ . She's ²_____ her homework, and her cat Sammy ³_____ sleeping on her bed. Her two brothers ⁴_____ watching a baseball game in the ⁵_____ room, and her sister is ⁶_____ a book ⁷_____ the yard. Their parents ⁸_____ here because ⁹_____ visiting some friends this afternoon.

| 9 |

2 Choose the correct answers

(Circle) the correct answer: a, b or c.

1 Dad's in the _____ . He's taking a shower.
   a (bathroom) b kitchen c dining room

2 There's a new _____ in the kitchen.
   a bed b sofa c stove

3 Put the milk in the _____ , please.
   a fridge b bath c toilet

4 Helen is in Mexico. She's _____ a great time.
   a doing b having c making

5 Don't turn off the TV. Jack and I _____ watching this game show.
   a am b is c are

6 Listen! Susan _____ the violin.
   a play b plays c 's playing

7 _____ the computer now?
   a Are you use b You're using c Are you using

8 What _____ today?
   a 's the weather like b 's the weather liking
   c does the weather like

9 John and Alex are talking, but Pauline _____ listening.
   a aren't b isn't c not

| 8 |

3 Vocabulary

Underline the word that is different from the others.

1 armchair   sofa   <u>bed</u>

2 yard   bedroom   kitchen

3 fridge   shower   bath

4 shower   stove   fridge

5 window   kitchen   living room

6 table   chair   stairs

7 garage   door   window

8 shelf   pillow   blanket

9 floor   hanger   ceiling

| 8 |

How did you do?

Total: | 25 |

| 😊 | Very good 25 – 20 | 😐 | OK 19 – 16 | 😞 | Review Unit 12 again 15 or less |

13 Special days

1 Remember and check

Complete the sentences with the words in the box.
Then check on page 86 of the Student's Book.

> blouses bread celebrate dancing dinner holiday
> ~~poet~~ skirt

- Every year on January 25, the Scots remember the famous
  1 _____poet_____ Robert Burns. There is usually a special
  2 _____ , and people eat a dish called haggis.

- Hogmanay is an important 3 _____ for the Scottish people.
  It is on December 31, and people 4 _____ with a party.
  They visit the homes of their friends and take a piece of
  5 _____ and a piece of coal.

- At the Highland Games, men wear kilts (a kind of 6 _____)
  and women wear skirts, 7 _____ and scarves. The bands play
  music, and there is 8 _____ .

2 Vocabulary

✳ Months of the year and seasons

a Fill in the puzzle with months of the year (1–9).
What's the other month (10)?

b Which two months aren't in the puzzle?

----

c Answer the questions.

1 What month is your birthday?

----

2 What month is your mother's birthday?

----

3 Name a month when you don't go to school.

----

4 Which months are cold in your country?

----

5 Which is your favorite month? Why?

----

d What do you do in each season?
Write a sentence for each season.

*In the winter, I play basketball, and I
sometimes go skiing.*

----

3 Grammar

✱ Prepositions

Complete the paragraph with *in, on* or *at*.

In my country, the school year begins ¹_____ February. My school day starts ²_____ 8:40, so I get up ³_____ 7:00. That's fine when the weather's nice, but it isn't so good ⁴_____ the winter. There are usually seven classes a day, but ⁵_____ Wednesday we always play sports in the afternoon. School finishes at 3:45, but ⁶_____ Thursdays I stay until 5:00 to play volleyball with the team. We have a long vacation ⁷_____ the summer. It begins ⁸_____ December and ends in February. I usually go away with my family for two weeks ⁹_____ January.

4 Vocabulary

✱ Clothes

a Put the letters in the correct order to make words for clothes. Write the words in the boxes.

| osehs   serds   tkejac   risht   anjes   westare   ranseeks   opt   snapt   cossk   frasc   ~~hitTrs~~ |

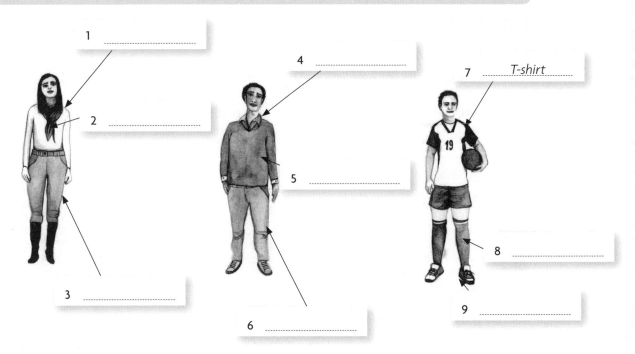

1 _____

2 _____

3 _____

4 _____

5 _____

6 _____

7 _____ *T-shirt* _____

8 _____

9 _____

b Write true answers to these questions.

1 What do you usually wear to school?

_____

2 What are your favorite clothes?

_____

3 What clothes do you hate wearing?

_____

4 What does your best friend usually wear?

_____

5 Where do you buy your clothes?

_____

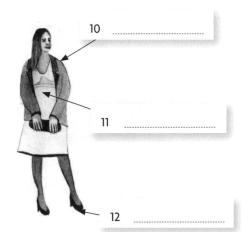

10 _____

11 _____

12 _____

Vocabulary bank <u>Underline</u> the word that is different from the others.

1 hat   cap   <u>tank top</u>   4 sandals   boots   shorts
2 suit   boots   tank top   5 socks   suit   shoes
3 T-shirt   shorts   pants

5 Pronunciation

✱ /æ/ and /ɛ/

a ▶ **CD3 T47** Listen to the word pairs and repeat.

	/æ/		/ɛ/	
1	sad	☐	said	☐
2	bad	☐	bed	☐
3	man	☐	men	☐
4	dad	☐	dead	☐
5	sat	☐	set	☐

b ▶ **CD3 T48** Listen to the sentences. Check (✔) the word you hear on the lists in Exercise 5a.

c ▶ **CD3 T49** Now listen to these sentences and repeat.

1 Annie is Alan's best friend.
2 I'm helping Joanna in December and January.
3 Emma's jacket is black and yellow.
4 How many magazines is Danny sending?

6 Grammar

✱ can/can't (asking for permission)

a **Write questions asking for permission. Then complete the answers with the words in the box.**

> They're really expensive.   I'm using it.   What's the problem?   Here you go.
> ~~What size?~~   We have visitors.

1 try on / sneakers?
A: _Can I try on those sneakers?_
B: Yes, of course. _What size?_

2 borrow / dictionary?
A: _____
B: Sorry, not right now.

3 come over / your house
A: _____
B: No, sorry. I'm busy.

4 see / homework?
A: _____
B: Yes, OK.

5 wear / sunglasses?
A: _____
B: No, you can't.

6 talk to / you?
A: _____
B: Yes, of course.

✱ one/ones

b Complete the sentences with *one* or *ones*.

1 Mom, my jeans are really old. Can I have some new
   ___ones___ ?

2 Can I see the shirt in the window, please? Um, the blue
   _____ ?

3 A: I love TV game shows.
   B: Me, too! Which _____ is your favorite?

4 A: I like your ski jacket.
   B: Thanks. It's a new _____ . It's nice, isn't it?

5 A: I'd like two kilos of apples, please.
   B: Certainly. Would you like these green _____ ?
   A: No, the red _____ , please.

6 A: Those two people are from Sweden.
   B: Which _____ ?
   A: The _____ in the corner, next to John and Linda.

7 Culture in mind

a Match the words to make phrases. Then check on page 91 of the Student's Book.

1 huge ⌐   a bands
2 jazz | b pastry
3 Zydeco ⌐── c celebration
4 colorful   d music
5 thick   e masks
6 fried   f soup

8 Study help
✱ Punctuation

a Which of these need a capital letter at the beginning of the word? Check (✔) the boxes.

1 names of places ☐
2 names of people ☐
3 days of the week ☐
4 months ☐
5 seasons ☐
6 color adjectives ☐
7 nationalities ☐

b Which words need to start with a capital letter? Correct them.

B
b̶ritain

friday

dave

fall

japanese

yellow

august

spring

tuesday

april

To help you remember, you can write the capital letter in a different color in your Vocabulary notebook.

b Use the phrases from 7a to complete these sentences.

1 The New Orleans Mardi Gras is a *huge celebration* .

2 _____ has a fast beat.

3 Gumbo is a _____ .

4 A beignet is a _____ .

5 During Mardi Gras people wear _____ .

6 In New Orleans people like to listen to
   _____ .

Skills in mind

9 Listen

▶ CD3 T50 Listen to Natalia talking to a woman in a clothing store.
Circle the correct answer: a, b or c.

1	the thing Natalia wants	a	dress	b	shirt	c	sweater
2	color	a	black	b	yellow	c	green
3	price	a	$49	b	$59	c	$79
4	Natalia's size	a	10	b	12	c	16
5	the thing she tries on	a	top	b	pants	c	jeans

10 Read

Read the text. Write words for clothes and colors on the lines.

> **READING TIP**
>
> *Reading for specific information*
>
> Exercise 10 asks you to find information from the text about the photos.
>
> - There are four photos. Find the part of the text that tells you about each one.
>
> - Look for key words in the text. In this exercise, the key words are clothes and colors.

Clothes in New York City

New York City is one of the world's centers for fashion, and people there wear all kinds of clothes. But some people wear special clothes at work. Here are some examples.

Between 1993 and 2005, there was popular TV show called *NYPD Blue*. NYPD stands for New York Police Department. Why "Blue"? That's because New York City police officers are famous for their blue uniforms. They wear dark blue hats, jackets, shirts and pants.

New York hotels like to give their guests a special welcome. When guests arrive, the doorman is there to say hello. Doormen usually wear very formal uniforms. At one famous New York hotel, the doormen wear special hats and beautiful red jackets.

Other New Yorkers wear work clothes to be safe. Men and women who work in the New York City subway have dangerous jobs. They wear bright orange vests because it helps the train drivers see them.

The business center of New York is Wall Street. These days, people in New York often wear jeans or even sneakers to work in some offices. This is not true on Wall Street. There men and women wear suits, and traditional colors like gray and dark blue are the most popular.

1   *a dark blue hat*

2   _____

3   _____

4   _____

Unit check

1 Fill in the blanks

Complete the sentences with the words in the box.

| at | in | festival | huge | clothes | enjoy | ~~party~~ | shorts | costume | parade |

I have a photo here of me and my friends at Carlo's carnival ___party___ . Everyone's wearing crazy
¹_____ . Carlo's wearing a strange red ²_____ , and Felicia has on black ³_____ and
a ⁴_____ hat. The carnival is ⁵_____ April every year, and it's a big ⁶_____ in
my town. There's a ⁷_____ in the streets. It starts ⁸_____ seven o'clock and lasts all evening.
We all really ⁹_____ it.

| 9 |

2 Choose the correct answers

Circle the correct answer: a, b or c.

1 We don't wear scarves and _____ in hot
   weather.
   a T-shirts b (sweaters) c jeans

2 He's wearing a white shirt and a black
   _____ .
   a socks b pants c hat

3 A: Mom, can I buy some new jeans?
   B: No, _____ .
   a you can't b you can c I can't

4 The month after March is _____ .
   a February b April c June

5 _____ I look at your magazine, please?
   a Am b Can c Do

6 I like the red shoes, not the blue _____ .
   a once b one c ones

7 Meet me _____ eleven thirty.
   a at b in c on

8 _____ is my favorite season.
   a July b Fall c August

9 A: I can't help you right now. Sorry.
   B: _____ .
   a Just a moment b Here you are
   c That's OK

| 8 |

3 Vocabulary

Find eight more words for clothes in the
wordsnake. (There are three more words
that are not clothes.) Write the words on
the lines below.

dressbootsjacketscarfneckeyebeltsandalsshirttopsockshair

1 ___dress___
2 _____
3 _____
4 _____
5 _____
6 _____
7 _____
8 _____
9 _____

| 8 |

How did you do?

Total: | 25 |

| ☺ Very good
25 – 20 | ☺ OK
19 – 16 | ☹ Review Unit 13 again
15 or less |

14) He was only 22.

1) Remember and check

Match the questions and answers about Buddy Holly. Then check on page 92 of the Student's Book.

1 Where was Buddy on February 3, 1959?   a They were singers and musicians.

2 Who was with him?   b Seventeen.

3 Who were the three men?   c In a plane in the state of Iowa.

4 What was the weather like?   d Four.

5 How many people died in the plane crash?   e Richie Valens and the Big Bopper.

6 How old was Richie Valens?   f It was very cold, with a lot of snow and wind.

2) Grammar

* Simple past: *was/wasn't; were/weren't*

a Complete the texts about these famous people. Use *was* or *were*.

Selena [1] *was* a Mexican-American singer from the state of Texas. Her full name [2] _____ Selena Quintanilla-Perez. She [3] _____ a beautiful woman, and her songs [4] _____ very popular. People all around the world [5] _____ very sad when she died in 1995. She [6] _____ only 23 years old.

Steve Irwin [7] _____ from Australia. Steve's nickname [8] _____ the Crocodile Hunter. He [9] _____ famous for his documentary programs about Australian animals. His wife Terri and daughter Bindi [10] _____ also part of the programs. Steve's work [11] _____ exciting, but it [12] _____ dangerous, too. He died in an accident in 2006. He [13] _____ only 44. Bindi is now continuing her father's work.

b Correct the statements about the people in 2a.

1 Selena was from Mexico.
   No, she wasn't. She was from Texas.

2 She was an actress.
   ....

3 People were very happy when she died.
   ....

4 Steve Irwin was an American.
   ....

5 His TV programs were soap operas.
   ....

6 Steve was 24 years old when he died.
   ....

C Look at the pictures and the times. Write questions and answers in the simple past.

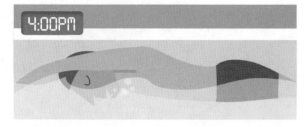

1 Joe / the station / four o'clock?

   A: *Was Joe at the station at four o'clock?*

   B: *No, he wasn't.*

2 Jane and Diana / the park / 2:30?

   A: _____

   B: _____

3 Julia / her bedroom / nine o'clock?

   A: _____

   B: _____

4 Paul and Carol / the supermarket / 10:15?

   A: _____

   B: _____

5 Anna / the bookstore / 5:30?

   A: _____

   B: _____

6 Matt / the kitchen / one o'clock?

   A: _____

   B: _____

3 Vocabulary

✱ Time expressions

a Complete the sentences with *last* or *yesterday*.

1 The bus was late  *yesterday* afternoon.

2 My aunt and uncle were in Caracas _____ week.

3 All my friends were at Karen's birthday party _____ weekend.

4 The library wasn't open _____ evening.

5 There was a good show on TV _____ night.

6 We were late for school _____ .

b Write true answers to these questions.

1 Where were you at 8:15 yesterday morning?

_____

2 Where were you at 5:00 p.m. last Friday?

_____

3 Were you in bed at 10 o'clock last night?

_____

4 Were you and your friends at school yesterday?

_____

5 Was your friend at your house last weekend?

_____

6 What day was your birthday last year?

_____

4 Remember and check

▶ **CD3 T51** Complete this part of the conversation from Exercise 5 of the Student's Book. Use *was*, *wasn't*, *were* or *weren't*. Then listen and check.

Grandma: Oh, I love this song.

Tom: I think I know it, Grandma. Is it the Beatles?

Grandma: That's right. They ¹_____ my favorite group.

Tom: Oh, right. ²_____ they from London?

Grandma: No, they ³_____! They ⁴_____ from Liverpool. Oh, they ⁵_____ fantastic, just wonderful.

Tom: How many of them ⁶_____ there, in the Beatles, I mean?

Grandma: There ⁷_____ four of them: John Lennon, Paul McCartney, George Harrison and Ringo Starr. They ⁸_____ very young, and I ⁹_____ very young, too! John ¹⁰_____ my favorite, but they ¹¹_____ all great. All the girls in my school ¹²_____ crazy about them!

Tom: Cool! Are their songs still on the radio?

Grandma: Yes, they are. That song "Yesterday," for example. That's a really famous Beatles song. They play that on the radio a lot.

5 Pronunciation

✱ *was/wasn't* and *were/weren't*

a ▶ **CD3 T52** Listen and repeat. <u>Underline</u> the words that are stressed.

1 Were they in <u>Boston</u>?	<u>Yes</u>, they <u>were</u>.
2 Were they happy?	No, they weren't.
3 Were the girls at home?	Yes, they were.
4 Was he an actor?	Yes, he was.
5 Was she worried?	No, she wasn't.
6 Was Dave at school?	No, he wasn't.

b ▶ **CD3 T53** <u>Underline</u> the words that you think are stressed. Then listen again, check and repeat.

1 Helen was in the hospital on Wednesday.
2 Our parents were at the library yesterday.
3 When were you in Paris?
4 What was your address?

6 Vocabulary

✱ Ordinal numbers and dates

a Complete the table.

4	four	4th	fourth
12	twelve	_____	_____
_____	_____	_____	second
_____	_____	_____	fifteenth
3	_____	_____	_____
1	_____	_____	_____
50	_____	50th	_____
22	twenty-two	_____	_____
31	_____	_____	_____

b Answer the questions.

1 What's the sixth month of the year?

   ....

2 What's the ninth month?

   ....

3 What's the last day of the school week?

   ....

4 What's the second day of the weekend?

   ....

5 What's your first class on Wednesday?

   ....

c Write sentences with the dates as we say them.

1 Sheila's birthday / May 17

   Sheila's birthday is on May seventeenth.

2 Our national holiday / July 4

   ....

3 first day of winter / December 21

   ....

4 New Year's Day / January 1

   ....

5 The festival / October 9

   ....

6 My party / August 30 / last year

   ....

7 Everyday English

Put the phrases in the box into the correct places.

| poor you   my fault   you know   suddenly |

1 **A:** There was a problem with the electricity last night.

   B: I know. I was in my bedroom, and .... it was dark!

2 **A:** Where's Antonia?

   B: She's upstairs in the bathroom, ... , taking a shower.

3 **A:** Look at the kitchen floor, Sophie! It's very dirty.

   B: Well, it isn't .... ! It was James. He was in the kitchen this afternoon.

4 **A:** I was in the hospital yesterday. I had an accident.

   B: .... ! Are you OK now?

8 Study help

★ Reviewing

To review new words, it's a good idea to make flash cards.

- Write a word on one side of the card and a picture, definition or translation on the other side. Use the cards to test yourself, or ask another person to test you.

- Put flash cards up around your room: on the walls, on the door, on your furniture. If you see the words often, they are easier to remember.

Find some important words in Unit 14. Write them here. Then write the words on real cards. Put the word on side A and a picture, definition or translation on side B.

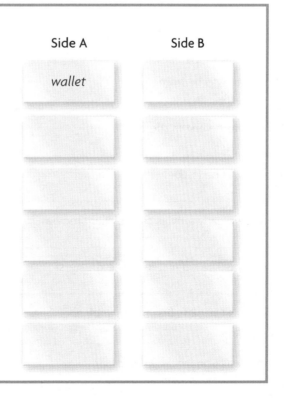

Side A   Side B

wallet

9 Listen

▶ **CD3 T54** Listen to the dates. Write the numbers 1–6.

a 03/03/2001 ☐   d 07/30/1995 ☐

b 11/25/1989 ☐   e 12/11/2010 ☐ 1

c 08/31/1999 ☐   f 09/13/1959 ☐

10 Read

Read the text and answer the questions.

Charlie Chaplin

Charlie Chaplin (1889–1977) was a very famous movie star. He was from a poor home in South London, and he was already a comedy actor in the theater when he was a teenager.

He went to the U.S. in 1910, and in 1914, he was in his first Hollywood movie. In those days, the movie industry was very young. Chaplin's early comedies were in black and white, and they were "silent." There were no words or music.

Chaplin's favorite character was "the tramp," a little man with big pants, an old black hat and a sad face. This was Chaplin's character in his famous comedy movies, for example, *The Kid* (1920), *The Gold Rush* (1924) and *City Lights* (1931). *Modern Times* (1936) was his first "talking" movie or "talkie." Then in *The Great Dictator* he was the director and music writer as well as the star.

Chaplin decided to leave the U.S. in 1952. His new home was in Switzerland. He died there on December 25, 1977, at the age of 88.

1 What nationality was Charlie Chaplin?
British.

2 What city was he from?

3 When was he first in the U.S.?

4 Where was he in 1914?

5 Why were early movies called "silent movies"?

6 When was *The Kid* first in movie theaters?

7 What was Chaplin's first talking movie?

8 Where was Chaplin when he died?

READING TIP

Answering questions

Make sure you know what the questions are asking. Study the question words.

- If the question asks *When ...?*, the answer is a date or a time.
- If it asks *Where ...?*, the answer is a place.
- If it asks *Why ...?*, the answer is a reason (*Because ...*).

Unit check

1 Fill in the blanks

Complete the sentences with the words in the box.

| was   were   wasn't   weren't   afternoon   ~~yesterday~~   fifth   way   first   recording |

Richard Deane is a piano player and a music teacher. At 10:00 __yesterday__ morning his ¹_____
music student was at the door, and there ²_____ two others at 11:00 and 12:30. Richard
³_____ hungry, but there ⁴_____ time for lunch. At 1:45, he was on his ⁵_____
to downtown Los Angeles in a taxi. At two o'clock in the ⁶_____ he and his band were in the
⁷_____ studio. But at the end of the day they ⁸_____ very happy. Their first four songs
were OK, but the ⁹_____ one wasn't very good.

9

2 Choose the correct answers

(Circle) the correct answer: a, b or c.

1   05/22 is May _____.
   a twenty-two   b (twenty-second)   c twentieth-two

2   Her birthday is _____ March 16.
   a in   b on   c at

3   Kate was in Brazil _____ 2009.
   a in   b on   c at

4   Today is my father's _____ birthday.
   a forty   b fourteenth   c fortieth

5   Jack's cousins _____ in Japan last year.
   a are   b were   c was

6   I _____ angry with you last week.
   a wasn't   b were   c weren't

7   _____ there a lot of children at the beach?
   a Is   b Were   c Was

8   Where _____ at four o'clock yesterday?
   a you were   b you was   c were you

9   I was sick _____ afternoon.
   a last   b yesterday   c before

8

3 Vocabulary

Write the letters in the correct order to make words.

1   I was in Paris last *kewe*. _____*week*_____

2   My dad's birthday is November *dihtr*. _____

3   I didn't feel well yesterday *oginmrn*. _____

4   My birthday is on April *venhtse*. _____

5   We always go on vacation in *stuAgu*. _____

6   I was at my friend's house yesterday *fonterano*. _____

7   I love *nuarJya*. In my country, it's vacation time. _____

8   Where were you last *thing*? _____

9   Today is March *wtntiteeh*. _____

8

How did you do?

Total: **25**

| ☺ | Very good 25 – 20 | ☺ | OK 19 – 16 | ☹ | Review Unit 14 again 15 or less |

15 What happened?

1 Remember and check

Complete the summary of the text about Rosa Parks. Use the adjectives in the box. Then check with the text on page 100 of the Student's Book.

angry   black   ~~full~~   little   tired   white   white

One day in December 1955, Rosa Parks got on a bus and sat down. Soon the bus was _____*full*_____ . The driver said to Rosa: "Give this man your seat!" Rosa was [1] _____ , so she said: "No."

When Rosa was a [2] _____ girl, she walked to school, but the [3] _____ children took a bus. Rosa went to a black school and studied with black children.

When Rosa said "No" on the bus, she broke the law because a [4] _____ person had to give their seat to a [5] _____ person. The police took Rosa to prison. Black people in Alabama were [6] _____ , and they stopped using the buses. Then the law changed, and this changed the U.S. forever.

2 Grammar

✱ Simple past: regular verbs

a Complete the table.

Verb	Simple past
1 work	*worked*
2 change	
3 hate	
4 study	
5 die	
6 listen	
7 walk	
8 start	

b Complete the dialogues. Use five of the simple past verbs in Exercise 2a.

1 **Dad:** Was the TV show good?
   Tony: No. I _____*hated*_____ it.

2 **Monica:** Are we late?
   Peter: Yes, the class _____ at 9:00 a.m.

3 **Dave:** Was Rosa Parks a teacher?
   Peggy: I don't think so. I think she _____ in a factory.

4 **Tom:** What were you up to last night?
   Fiona: Nothing much. I _____ for the English test at home.

5 **Lee:** Were you on the school bus yesterday?
   Chris: No, we _____ to school.

6 **Martin:** Sandra looks sad. Do you know why?
   Jane: Yes, her uncle _____ last week.

3 Pronunciation

✱ -ed endings

a ▶ **CD3 T55** Write the verbs in the lists. Then listen and check.

/t/ or /d/	/ɪd/
liked	*hated*

~~liked~~ ~~hated~~ changed called
started landed watched wanted

b ▶ **CD3 T56** Listen and repeat. Make sure you say /ɪd/ for the -ed sound.

1 They visited a museum.

2 They landed on the moon.

3 The concert ended at 11 o'clock.

4 We waited at the station.

c ▶ **CD3 T57** Listen and repeat. Is the -ed sound /t/ or /d/? Write /t/ or /d/ in the spaces.

1 We watched the game. /t/

2 He lived in Quito. ....

3 We helped Annie with her homework. ....

4 They laughed at me. ....

5 Sally stayed in a hotel. ....

6 We opened our books. ....

4 Grammar

✱ Simple past: irregular verbs

a Fill in the crossword with the simple past forms of the verbs.

Across	Down
1 leave	2 find
3 become	3 begin
4 eat	6 write
5 know	8 go
7 see	10 have
9 run	12 get
11 think	
13 give	
14 take	

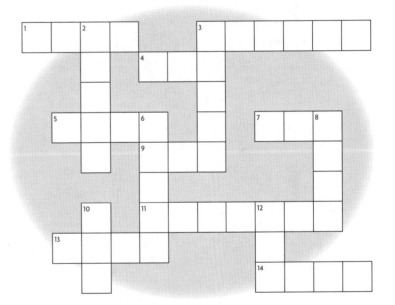

b What did Angela do on Saturday? Look at the pictures and complete the sentences.

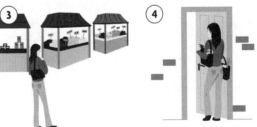

Angela ¹........................ at 8:30, and she ²........................ for a walk with her dog. After breakfast, she ³........................ to the market. She ⁴........................ home at 12:00, and then she ⁵........................ an email to her friend Zach. Angela and her family ⁶........................ lunch at 1:15.

5 Grammar

✱ Simple past: affirmatives and negatives

a Write affirmative and negative sentences. Use the simple past.

1 (stay) Last summer, Julia ____*stayed in Paris*____ .
   She didn't stay in Rome.

2 (play) Last night, Ben and Adam _____

3 (work) In 2008, Alan _____

4 (call) Yesterday, I _____

5 (dance / watch) On Friday, we _____

6 (park) On Saturday, Lynn _____

b Complete the dialogue with the simple past. Use the verbs in parentheses.

Jason: What ____*did*____ you ____*do*____ (do) last night?

Sylvia: We ¹_____ (go) to the movies. We ²_____ (see) the new 3D movie.

Jason: What time ³_____ it _____ (start)?

Sylvia: At 6:30.

Jason: Where ⁴_____ you _____ (go) after the movie?

Sylvia: To the Riverview Restaurant.

Jason: ⁵_____ George _____ (have) dinner with you?

Sylvia: Yes, he did.

Jason: ⁶_____ you _____ (sit) outside?

Sylvia: No, it was a little cold, so we ⁷_____ (sit) inside.

Jason: What ⁸_____ you _____ (have) for dinner?

Sylvia: I ⁹_____ (have) fresh fish with potatoes and salad.

Jason: Was it good?

Sylvia: Yes, it was delicious.

Jason: When ¹⁰_____ you _____ (get) home?

Sylvia: At about 11:30.

6 Vocabulary

✱ Verb and noun pairs

a Complete the sentences with the correct form of *have, play* or *go to*.

1 Kevin and Tony are __playing__ tennis this afternoon.
2 Do you want to _____ Eva's party?
3 My cousin _____ the piano.
4 Can I _____ some ice cream?
5 Ari _____ a new cell phone.
6 We're _____ the gym.

b **Vocabulary bank** Write the words in the correct column.

a break   ~~a mistake~~   a noise   a picture   a puzzle   an accident   fun   housework

make	do	have	take
a mistake	....	....	....
....	....	....	....

7 Culture in mind

Match the two parts of the sentences. Check your answers with the text on page 104 of the Student's Book.

1 Gertrude Berg was born
2 At her father's resort, Gertrude
3 *The Goldbergs* was first
4 In 1949, *The Goldbergs*
5 The show was about
6 Gertrude Berg was

a became the first TV sitcom.
b a family living in New York City.
c in 1898 in New York City.
d the star and the director of the show.
e wrote plays for other children.
f a radio show.

8 Study help

✱ Spelling and pronunciation

a To remember the spelling rules for simple past verbs, you can group them like this in your Vocabulary notebook.

+ -ed
start – started
....
....

+ -d
love – loved
....
....

y + -ied
study – studied
....
....

double letter
shop – shopped
....
....

Add these words to the lists.

marry   answer   dance   stop   play
cry   hop   practice

b You can also group simple past verbs to show their pronunciation.

/t/	/d/	/ɪd/
helped	loved	started
....	....	....
....	....	....
....	....	....

Add the simple past form of these words to the lists.

hate   shop   want   ask   enjoy
watch   end   look   die

Skills in mind

9 Listen

▶ **CD3 T58** Antonio is on vacation in the U.S. with his father. Listen to his conversation with Samuel. Look at the pictures and (circle) the correct answer: A, B or C.

1 When did they arrive in Washington, D.C.?

Sunday	Monday	Tuesday
A	B	C

2 What time did the plane land?

A   B   C

3 Where did they stay on Tuesday?

A   B   C

4 What didn't they do in Washington, D.C.?

A   B   C

5 How did they get to Orlando?

A   B   C

> ### WRITING TIP
>
> *Writing an email to a friend*
>
> - You can start with *Dear* (*Carol*), but in emails people often say *Hi* (*Carol*).
>
> - Here are some endings you can use:
>   *Love,* (*from*)
>   *Bye.*
>   *See you soon.*
>   *Write soon.*

10 Write

Write a reply to Carol's email. Tell her about the information you heard in Exercise 9.

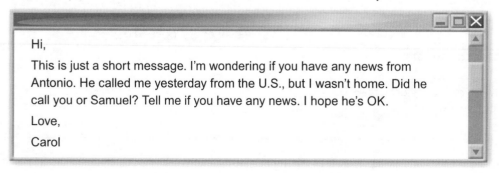

Hi,

This is just a short message. I'm wondering if you have any news from Antonio. He called me yesterday from the U.S., but I wasn't home. Did he call you or Samuel? Tell me if you have any news. I hope he's OK.

Love,

Carol

Unit check

1 Fill in the blanks

Complete the sentences with the words in the box.

| were | on | didn't | in | ~~born~~ | stopped | studied | died | hospital | nurse |

My grandmother was ____*born*____ in Germany [1]_____ February 18, 1944. Her family moved to Italy
[2]_____ 1960. She [3]_____ at the university in Milan, and later she became a [4]_____ .
She worked in a big [5]_____ in Bologna for four years, but after she was married, she [6]_____
working. She and my grandfather had five children. They [7]_____ have a lot of money, but they
[8]_____ very happy together. My grandmother [9]_____ in 2008. She was only 64. We still
miss her a lot.

9

2 Choose the correct answers

(Circle) the correct answer: a, b or c.

1 I'd like to _____ some soup.
   a practice   b play   c (have)

2 Alan goes to _____ every morning.
   a work   b a bath   c coffee

3 Andrew _____ the piano at the school concert.
   a had   b practiced   c played

4 The train _____ at 8:30 p.m.
   a arrived   b ended   c visited

5 Did she _____ a good time at the party?
   a has   b had   c have

6 The woman _____ open the door.
   a did   b didn't   c don't

7 What _____ last weekend?
   a you did   b do you did   c did you do

8 A: Did you talk to David yesterday?
   B: No, I _____ .
   a didn't   b doesn't   c don't

9 A: _____ did your cousins arrive?
   B: On Sunday.
   a Where   b When   c What

8

3 Vocabulary

(Circle) the correct answer: a, b or c.

1 My uncle _____ a bad accident last week.
   a (had)   b took   c did

2 My sister _____ a doctor in 2010.
   a become   b came   c became

3 Last weekend, we _____ to Boston.
   a go   b went   c gone

4 I _____ 15 emails yesterday evening.
   a wrote   b writing   c written

5 My sister _____ my laptop, and she didn't ask me!
   a take   b taked   c took

6 Oh, is Canberra the capital of Australia?
   I _____ it was Sydney.
   a think   b thank   c thought

7 Please don't _____ a lot of noise tonight.
   a make   b do   c have

8 I hate _____ housework!
   a doing   b making   c taking

9 Andy _____ some great pictures last week.
   a made   b took   c did

8

How did you do?

Total: **25**

| :) | Very good 25 – 20 | :| | OK 19 – 16 | :(| Review Unit 15 again 15 or less |

16 Things change.

1 Remember and check

a ▶ **CD3 T59** Think back to the exercise with Dave (*D*) and his grandmother (*G*) on page 106 of the Student's Book. Match the two parts of the sentences. Then listen and check your answers.

1 G: When I was young, of course,   a are difficult for my grandma.

2 G: I think school life is more   b cars these days.

3 G: I think people were   c difficult now, certainly.

4 D: Some things now   d faster than in the 1960s.

5 D: I'm sure that now, life is   e a lot of TV was in black-and-white!

6 D: There are a lot more   f friendlier in the 60s than they are now.

b Find pairs of opposites in the box.

> ~~exciting~~ young crowded different
> fast difficult empty happy slow
> ~~boring~~ sad easy the same old

exciting	*boring*
....	....
....	....
....	....
....	....
....	....
....	....

2 Grammar

✱ Comparative of adjectives

a Complete the table.

Adjective	Comparative adjective
1 hard	*harder*
2 hot	....
3 happy	....
4 difficult	....
5 unhappy	....
6 expensive	....
7 good	....
8 hungry	....
9 mysterious	....
10 bad	....

b Look at the picture and answer the questions. Write *A* or *B*.

1 Which dog is smaller?   *B*

2 Which one is older?   ....

3 Which one has longer ears?   ....

4 Which one has curlier hair?   ....

5 Which one is more excited?   ....

6 Which one do you think is nicer?   ....

c Read the information about Brian and Rebecca. Then complete the sentences. Use the comparative form of the adjectives in the box.

bad   high   tall   interesting   ~~young~~   big

Rebecca   Brian

	Rebecca	Brian
Age:	16	15
Height:	1.7 m	1.6 m
Brothers and sisters:	4	1
Math grades:	95%	85%
French grades:	52%	60%
Art project:		

1 Brian is 15. He's _____*younger*_____ than Rebecca.

2 Rebecca is 1.7 meters tall. She's _____ than Brian.

3 Rebecca's family is _____ than Brian's.

4 Rebecca's math grades are _____ than Brian's.

5 But her French grades are _____ than Brian's.

6 Brian's art project is _____ than Rebecca's.

d Look at the pictures and write sentences. Use the comparative form of the adjectives in parentheses.

1 (cold) *Today's colder than yesterday.*

2 (expensive) *The dress* _____
_____

3 (interesting) _____
_____

town   city

4 (busy) _____

5 (fast) _____
_____

CD   MP3

6 (good) _____
_____

e Write true sentences comparing these things.

1 me – my best friend

....
....
....

2 my street – my friend's street

....
....
....

3 my town – (another place)

....
....
....

4 school days – weekends

....
....
....

5 sitcoms – the news

....
....
....

6 history – English

....
....
....

3 Pronunciation

✳ than

▶ **CD3 T60** Listen to the sentences. <u>Underline</u> the words that are stressed. Listen again and repeat.

1 She's younger than Tom.
2 You're happier than Liz.
3 The bank is older than the bookstore.
4 Math is more difficult than science.
5 The book was more interesting than the movie.
6 The sandals were more expensive than the sneakers.

4 Vocabulary

✳ Adjectives and opposites

a Match the two parts of the sentences.

1 Some snakes   a be quiet.
2 I didn't finish the book because it   b look old-fashioned now.
3 She couldn't sleep because the traffic   c in a modern train.
4 We loved the tour. It   d was very noisy.
5 Don't climb on the roof. It   e isn't safe.
6 You can travel very fast   f are dangerous.
7 I'm watching this show, so please   g was boring.
8 Computers from the 1990s   h was really exciting.

b Complete the sentences. Use six of the adjectives from Exercise 4a.

1 It was an ....*exciting*.......... race.

2 A: Is this river .... for swimming?

   B: No! There are alligators here!

3 A: What is it?

   B: It's an .... washing machine.

4 They have a .... kitchen.

5 Don't go in there. It's ....

6 A: Oh! It's very .... !

   B: What? I can't hear you.

c **Vocabulary bank** Write the opposite adjectives in the spaces.

a young man   →   an ¹ ___old___ man

a friendly dog   →   a ² _____ dog

a ³ _____ window   →   a dirty window

a neat room   →   a ⁴ _____ room

a comfortable armchair   →   an ⁵ _____ armchair

a light computer   →   a ⁶ _____ computer

a ⁷ _____ dinner   →   a heavy dinner

a light color   →   a ⁸ _____ color

5 Everyday English

Complete the dialogues. Use one word from Box A and Box B each time.

A	B
what's	of
you	believe it
I don't	the matter
sort	see

1 **A:** Did you like that documentary on TV last night?

   B: Well, it was _____ interesting at first, but after 20 minutes I got bored.

2 **A:** You didn't come to my party on Saturday!

   B: I know. I'm sorry. _____ , my mother was sick, so I stayed at home to help her.

3 **A:** _____ , Sandy?

   B: I got some bad news about my uncle in the U.S.

4 **A:** Guess what? I asked Gloria to go to the game with me, and she said yes!

   B: _____ !

6 Study help

✱ Reviewing

When you're reviewing for a test, try working with a friend. Make tests for each other. For example:

- Write sentences with a mistake in each one. Correct the mistakes in your friend's sentences. Here's one to practice. Can you see the mistake?

  I'm older then my brother Ned.

- Write sentences and leave blanks for one or two words. Fill in the blanks in your friend's sentences. Here's one to practice.

  Our stove is _____ modern than the fridge.

Skills in mind

7 Listen

▶ **CD3 T61** Listen and write the names in the picture.

Tim   Frank   Anne   Lisa   Dad   Uncle Bill   Sandy   Pablo

4 _____

5 _____

2 _____

1 _____

3 _____

6 _____

7 _____

8 _____

LISTENING TIP

Reviewing

Use your Workbook recording to help you review. Practice the pronunciation exercises and listen to the dialogues.

- Play the recording often at home. For example, you can listen when you're getting dressed in the morning, or for 10 minutes before you go to sleep.

- If possible, play the recording when you're out. Listen on your way to school or when you're sitting in the bus.

8 Write

Write a paragraph comparing the two living rooms.

Alan's room is smaller than Peggy's, and it has more modern furniture ...

Alan's room

Peggy's room

Unit check

1 Fill in the blanks

Complete the sentences with the words in the box.

> difficult   busier   ~~lived~~   more   modern   crowded   easier   was   town   old-fashioned

My family ___*lived*___ in the city for a long time, but in 2006, we moved to an old house in a small
1_____ called Hancock. Of course it 2_____ strange at first. New York City was a lot
3_____ and 4_____ exciting than Hancock. We missed the 5_____ streets and the
big stores. In our house we had an 6_____ stove so it was 7_____ to cook, and there was only
one very small bathroom. But later, when we got a 8_____ kitchen and a larger bathroom, life was
9_____ . Now, we love the place.

| 9 |

2 Choose the correct answers

(Circle) the correct answer: a, b or c.

1 Helen is taller _____ Wendy.
   a that   b (than)   c then

2 This is a _____ road. There are a lot of accidents here.
   a quiet   b safe   c dangerous

3 That radio is 60 years old, so it's very _____ .
   a funny   b old-fashioned   c noisy

4 Sorry, I can't talk to you now. I'm very _____ .
   a busy   b important   c difficult

5 Joe is 12, so he's _____ than William.
   a younger   b newer   c more modern

6 This is terrible. The weather was awful yesterday, and today it's _____ .
   a bigger   b better   c worse

7 I was a _____ person before I came to this town.
   a more happy   b happier   c happyer

8 I'm _____ than my sister.
   a tall   b taller   c more tall

9 A: Great! This T-shirt's only $5.50.
   B: Yes, and the white one's _____ cheaper.
   a lot   b more   c even

| 8 |

3 Vocabulary

Choose a word from the box to complete each sentence. There are three words you do not need.

> dirty   light   dark   heavy   old-fashioned
> difficult   quiet   safe   young   exciting
> big   ~~easy~~

1 I'm not worried about the test today. I'm sure it's very ___*easy*___ .

2 The soccer game yesterday was great. It was very, very _____ ! The score was 5–4!

3 That's a very _____ question. I don't know the answer.

4 Look at that telephone. It's from 1985! Wow, that's really _____ now.

5 Please be _____ , Mike. I'm talking to someone on the phone!

6 I'm not really hungry. Can I have a very _____ meal, please? Salad, maybe?

7 Alex, can you clean the windows, please? They're _____ .

8 I'm sorry, I can't carry all these books. They're very _____ – about 10 kilos, I think!

9 Can you turn the lights on please? It's _____ in here! I can't read my book.

| 8 |

How did you do?

Total: | 25 |

😊	Very good 25 – 20
😐	OK 19 – 16
😟	Review Unit 16 again 15 or less

Vocabulary bank

Unit 3 countries and nationalities

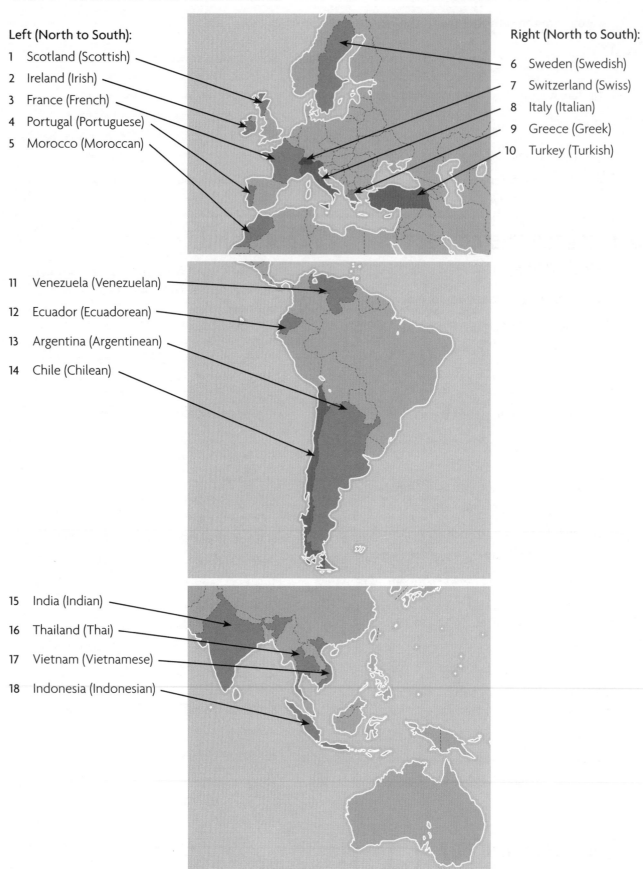

Left (North to South):
1   Scotland (Scottish)
2   Ireland (Irish)
3   France (French)
4   Portugal (Portuguese)
5   Morocco (Moroccan)

Right (North to South):
6   Sweden (Swedish)
7   Switzerland (Swiss)
8   Italy (Italian)
9   Greece (Greek)
10 Turkey (Turkish)

11 Venezuela (Venezuelan)
12 Ecuador (Ecuadorean)
13 Argentina (Argentinean)
14 Chile (Chilean)

15 India (Indian)
16 Thailand (Thai)
17 Vietnam (Vietnamese)
18 Indonesia (Indonesian)

Unit 4 affirmative and negative adjectives

Affirmative

1   It's a **wonderful** party.

2   This food is **delicious**.

3   She's a **terrific** singer.

Negative

4   It's a **horrible** party.

5   This food is **disgusting**

6   He's a **dreadful** singer.

Unit 5 family

Fred is Pauline's **father-in-law**.

Susan is Pauline's **mother-in-law**.

James is Pauline's **brother-in-law**.

Carol is Pauline's **sister-in-law**.

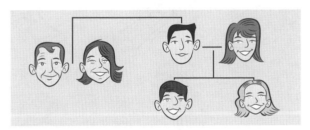

James is Stephen and Marion's **grandson**.

Nadia is Stephen and Marion's **granddaughter**.

James and Nadia are Stephen and Marion's **grandchildren**.

Stephen and Marion are James and Nadia's **grandparents**.

Unit 6 places in towns

1   a police station

2   a bus station

3   an elementary school

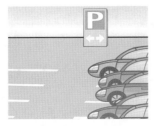

4   a high school

5   shopping mall

6   a parking lot

7   a department store

8   a gym

Unit 7 parts of the body

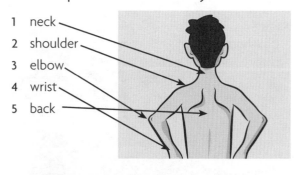

1 neck
2 shoulder
3 elbow
4 wrist
5 back

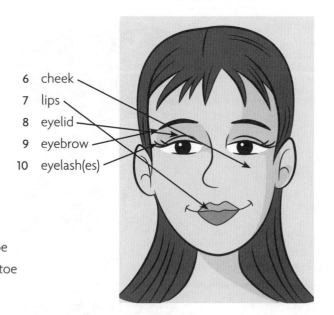

6 cheek
7 lips
8 eyelid
9 eyebrow
10 eyelash(es)

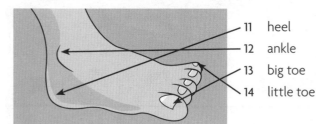

11 heel
12 ankle
13 big toe
14 little toe

Unit 8 food

1 fish 2 salt 3 pepper 4 cereal 5 olive oil

6 garlic 7 beans 8 yogurt 9 mushrooms 10 chocolate

Unit 10 adjectives to describe feelings

1 Mary feels very **stressed**. 2 James feels very **relaxed**. 3 Alex feels **sleepy**.

4 Sandra is very **upset**. 5 Gail is **cheerful**. 6 George is **frightened**.

Unit 11 sports

1 The **score** is **two–two**. It's **a tie**.

2 The **fans** are very happy!

3 The **referee** starts and ends the game.

4 It's the end of **the first quarter and the score is 1–nothing.**

5 It's the end of **the first half,** and the score is **two to one.**

6 It's the end of the **third quarter.** New York **is losing.** Los Angeles **is winning.**

7 Jones **came in first.** Smith **came in second.** Brown **came in third.**

8 Our team is great! We are the **champions.**

9 It's the end of the final quarter, and the score is 0–0. The game is going into **overtime.**

Unit 12 house and furniture

1 a **shelf** (*pl.* shelves)   2 a **chest of drawers**   3 **curtains**   4 **ceiling**   5 a **closet**   6 a [clothes] **hanger**

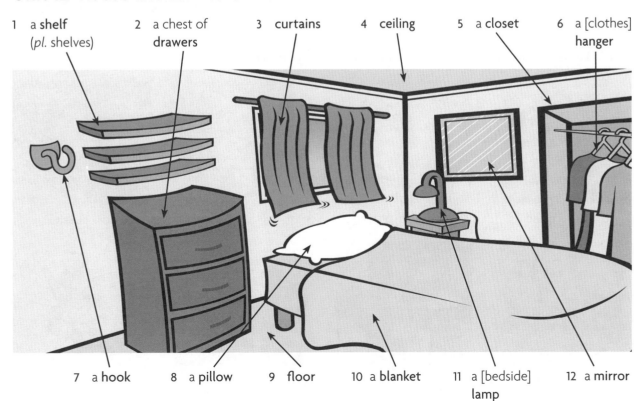

7 a **hook**   8 a **pillow**   9 **floor**   10 a **blanket**   11 a [bedside] **lamp**   12 a **mirror**

Unit 13 clothes

1 a **belt**

2 a **hat**

3 a **cap**

4 a **tank top**

5 a **suit**

6 a pair of **shorts**

7 a pair of **boots**

8 a pair of **sandals**

materials

9 COTTON T-SHIRTS ONLY $8.99!

10 SWEATERS 100% WOOL $29.99!

11 PLASTIC BELTS BLACK OR BROWN $5.99!

12 LEATHER JACKETS 25% OFF!

Unit 15 verb and noun pairs: *make/do/take/have*

1 to **make** a **noise**

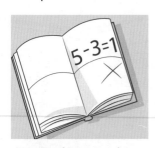

2 to **make** a mistake

3 to **do** the **housework**

4 to **do** a **puzzle**

5 to **take** a **picture**

6 to **take** a **break**

7 to **have** fun

8 to **have** an **accident**

Unit 16 adjectives and opposites

1 a **young** woman   2 an **old** woman

3 a **friendly** cat   4 a **mean** cat

5 a **clean** car   6 a **dirty** car

7 a **neat** desk   8 a **messy** desk

9 a **comfortable** sofa   10 an **uncomfortable** sofa

11 a **light** suitcase   12 a **heavy** suitcase

13 a **light** meal   14 a **heavy** meal

15 a **light** room   16 a **dark** room

Grammar reference

Units 3 and 4

The verb *be*: singular, plural, negatives and questions

1   We form the simple present of *be* like this:

Singular	Plural
I am	*we are*
you are	*you are*
he/she/it is	*they are*

2   In speaking and informal writing, we use short forms.

   I'm   you're   he's   she's   it's   we're   they're

3   We use the verb *be* before a noun or an adjective.

   *He's an **actor**.   They're **soccer players**.   I'm **American**.*

4   We make the negative by adding *not*.

   *I am **not**   you are **not***

   In speaking and informal writing, we use short forms.

   *I'm **not**   you **aren't**   he **isn't**   she **isn't**   it **isn't**   we **aren't**   they **aren't***

5   To make questions, we put the verb before the subject.

***Am I** right?*	*Yes, you **are**. / No, you **aren't**.*
***Are you** American?*	*Yes, I **am**. / No, I'm **not**.*
***Is he** an actor?*	*Yes, he **is**. / No, he **isn't**.*
***Is she** from Brazil?*	*Yes, she **is**. / No, she **isn't**.*
***Are we** late?*	*Yes, we **are**. / No, we **aren't**.*
***Are they** singers?*	*Yes, they **are**. / No, they **aren't**.*

Unit 3

wh- question words

Who ...?	questions ask about a person/people.
	***Who** are they? They're my friends.*
What ...?	questions ask about a thing/things.
	***What's** this? It's a computer game.*
When ...?	questions ask about a time.
	***When's** the concert? It's at seven o'clock.*
	***When's** your music class? It's on Monday.*
Where ...?	questions ask about a place.
	***Where's** Quito? It's in Ecuador.*
How old ...?	questions ask about age.
	***How old** are you? I'm 15.*
How many ...?	questions ask about a number.
	***How many** students are in your class? Twenty-six.*

Unit 4

Object pronouns

1   Here is a list of pronouns.

Subject	*I you he she it we they*
Object	*me you him her it us them*

2 We use object pronouns after the verb, instead of a noun.

*I like **the music**.*   *– I like **it**.*
*I love **my mother**.*   *– I love **her**.*
*They don't like **you and me**.*   *– They don't like **us**.*
*I want to see **Jack and Sue**.*   *– I want to see **them**.*

Unit 5

Simple present

1 We use the simple present for things that happen regularly or are normally true.

*We **watch** TV after school.*   *He **goes** shopping at the supermarket.*
*They **live** in Australia.*   *She **speaks** French.*

2 Usually the simple present is the same as the base form of the verb. But with a third-person singular subject (*he, she, it*), we use an -*s* ending.

*I **play** tennis.*   *She **plays** tennis.*
*My parents **work** in New York.*   *My brother **works** in New York.*

If a verb ends with *o, sh, ch, ss* or *x*, we add *es*.

*go – it go**es**   finish – he finish**es**   watch – she watch**es**   miss – he miss**es**   fix – she fix**es***

If a verb ends with consonant + *y*, we change the *y* to *i* and add *es*.

*study – she stud**ies**   carry – he carr**ies**   fly – it fl**ies***

3 We make the negative with *don't* (*do not*) or *doesn't* (*does not*) + base form of the verb.

*I **don't like** soccer.*   *He **doesn't like** soccer.*
*My cousins **don't live** in Mexico.*   *Daniela **doesn't live** in Mexico.*

4 We make questions with *Do* or *Does* + base form of the verb.

***Do** you **like** me?*   ***Does** Kate **go** to school?*
***Do** we **know** the answer?*   ***Does** he **listen** to the radio?*
***Do** your parents **work**?*   ***Does** this store **sell** chocolate?*

Possessive 's

1 We put *'s* after a noun to say who something belongs to.

Mom's car   John's family   Susan's bicycle
the dog's bed   my brother's problem   your sister's friend

2 We <u>don't</u> usually say ~~the family of John~~, ~~the car of my father~~, etc.

Possessive adjectives

1 Here is a list of possessive adjectives.

Subject pronoun	I	you	he	she	it	we	they
Possessive adjective	**my**	**your**	**his**	**her**	**its**	**our**	**their**

2 We use these adjectives before a noun to say who something belongs to.

***My** name's Steve.*   *I like **your** parents.*
*He's rich. Look at **his** car!*   *We love **our** dog.*
*She's a good teacher. We like **her** classes.*   *They ride **their** bicycles to school.*
*The DVD isn't in **its** case.*

Unit 6

There's / there are

1 We use *there's / there are* to say that something exists.

***There's** a bank on South Street.*
***There are** two parks in my town.*   ***There are** a lot of good restaurants here.*

2 The full form of *there's* is *there is*. In speaking and informal writing, we usually say *there's*.

3 In affirmative sentences, we use *there's* + *a/an* + singular noun and *there are* + plural noun.

***There's a** package on the table.*

*There's **an** interesting movie on TV.*
*There **are** good clothes at the store.*

4   In questions and negative sentences, we use *a/an* + singular noun and *any* + plural noun.
   ***Is there** a train station here?*   *There **isn't** a train station here.*
   ***Are there** any cafés on this street?*   *There **aren't** any cafés on this street.*

Affirmative imperative

1   We use the imperative when we want to tell someone to do something.

2   The affirmative imperative is the same as the base form of the verb.
   ***Turn** left onto Spring Street.   **Sit** down on that chair.   **Be** quiet, please!*

Prepositions of place

We use prepositions of place to say where something or someone is.
*My pen is **in** my bag.*
*The box is **on** the table.*
*Our car is **in front of** the post office.*
*There's a yard **behind** the house.*
*There's a table **next to** my bed.*
*The bookstore is **between** the drugstore and the newsstand.*

Unit 7

Why ...? Because ...

Why ...? questions ask about the reason for something that happens. We usually answer the question with *Because ...*
***Why** do you want to see this band?*   ***Because** their music is fantastic.*

has/have

1   We use the verb *have* to talk about things that people own.

2   Normally we use *have*. But with a third-person singular subject (*he, she, it*) we use *has*.
   *I **have** two brothers.*   *Ben **has** a new computer.*
   *They **have** a DVD player.*   *My sister **has** blonde hair.*

3   The negative form is *don't have / doesn't have*.
   *You **don't have** a big family.*   *Alison **doesn't have** a cell phone.*
   *We **don't have** a computer at home.*   *My brother **doesn't have** blond hair.*

4   To make questions we use *Do/Does* + subject + *have*.
   ***Do** you **have** a bicycle?*   ***Does** she **have** blue eyes?*
   ***Do** we **have** a problem?*   ***Does** your uncle **have** a car?*

Unit 8

Count and noncount nouns

1   Nouns in English are count or noncount. Count nouns have a singular and a plural form.
   apple – apples   tomato – tomatoes   book – books   question – questions   man – men

2   Noncount nouns don't have a plural form. They are always singular.
   food fruit rice bread milk music money hair homework
   *This **food is** delicious.   The **music is** awful!   Your **hair is** beautiful.   My **homework is** in my bag.*

3   Some nouns can be count or noncount.
   *I want to buy two **chickens** at the supermarket.   (= two whole birds, countable)*
   *Roast **chicken** is my favorite meal.   (= a type of meat, noncount)*

4   With count nouns, we can use *a/an* + singular noun and *some* + plural noun.
   *There's **a café** next to the movie theater.   I'd like **some strawberries**.*
   *I often have **an egg** for breakfast.   There are **some** good **CDs** in that store.*

5   With noncount nouns, we use *some*.

    *I'm hungry. I want **some food**.*   *Please buy **some milk** at the supermarket.*

    We <u>don't</u> use *a/an* with noncount nouns ~~*a bread*~~   ~~*an information*~~

this/that/these/those

1   We use *this* or *that* + singular noun. We use *these* or *those* + plural noun.

    this *egg*   **that** *book*   **these** *clothes*   **those** *apples*

2   We use *this* or *these* to point out things that are close to us. We use *that* or *those* to point out things that are at some distance from us.

    *Come and look at **this** letter.*   *Mmm! **These** strawberries are delicious.*

    ***That** man on the corner is our teacher.*   *Can you see **those** people over there?*

I'd like … / Would you like …?

1   We use *would like* to ask for things or to offer things. *Would like* is more polite than *want*.

    ***I'd like** two kilos of apples, please.*   ***Would** you **like** vegetables with your meal?*

2   The full form of *I'd like* is *I would like*, but in speaking and informal writing, we use the short form.

Unit 9

Adverbs of frequency

1   Adverbs of frequency are words that say how often we do things.

    always   usually   often   sometimes   hardly ever   never

2   Adverbs of frequency come <u>after</u> the verb *be*, but <u>before</u> other verbs.

    *I'm **usually** tired after school.*   *I **usually have** breakfast at 7:30.*

    *He's **always** late.*   *She **always arrives** before me.*

    *We're **never** bored.*   *We **never go** to that restaurant.*

Unit 10

Negative imperatives

We form the negative imperative with *Don't* + base form of the verb.

    ***Don't buy** those eggs. They aren't fresh.*   ***Don't cry.** It's OK.*   ***Don't** worry!*

Unit 11

can/can't (ability)

1   We use *can/can't* to talk about someone's ability to do something. The form is *can/can't* + base form of the verb.

    *I **can swim** 3 kilometers.*   *My little sister **can count** to 100.*   *We **can walk** on our hands.*

    *They **can't run** fast.*   *My father **can't ride** a horse.*   *We **can't speak** Chinese.*

2   To make questions we use *Can* + subject + base form of the verb.

    ***Can** your brother **swim**?*   ***Can** you **use** a computer?*   ***Can** they **play** the violin?*

    We <u>don't</u> use the verb *do* for questions or negatives.

like / don't like + *-ing*

1   We often use the *-ing* form of a verb after *like, enjoy, love* and *hate*.

    He likes cycling.   *I love swimming.*   *They enjoy watching tennis.*

    Anne doesn't like skiing.   *She hates playing computer games.*

2   If a verb ends in *e*, we drop the *e* before adding *-ing*.

    live – living   ride – riding

    If a short verb ends in 1 vowel + 1 consonant, we double the final consonant before adding *-ing*.

    get – getting   shop – shopping   swim – swimming

    In American English, if a short verb ends in 1 vowel + *l*, we don't often double the final *l* before adding *-ing*.

    travel – traveling   *cancel – canceling*

Unit 12

Present continuous

1   We use the present continuous to talk about things happening at the moment of speaking.
    *The girls **are doing** their homework now.*
    *Alex is in the bathroom. He's **taking** a shower.*
    *Don't make a sound. I'm **listening** to the radio.*

2   We form the present continuous with the present simple of *be* + *-ing* form of the verb.
    *I'm **having** lunch.*   *You're **shouting**!*
    *He's **playing** volleyball.*   *We're **sitting** in the yard.*
    *It's **raining**.*   *They're **studying** in the library.*

3   We make questions and negatives with the question/negative form of *be* + *-ing* form of the verb.
    *I'm **not watching** TV.*   ***Are** you **speaking** to me?*
    *You **aren't listening** to me!*   ***Is** he **doing** his homework?*
    *She **isn't playing** well today.*   ***Are** they **traveling** in France?*

4   Some verbs aren't normally used in the present continuous, for example:
    understand   know   like   hate   remember   forget   want

5   Look at the difference between the present continuous and the simple present.
    *I usually **do** my homework in my bedroom, but today I'm **doing** it in the dining room.*
    *My father hardly ever **watches** TV, but this afternoon he's **watching** soccer.*
    *I **listen to** music every day. Right now, I'm **listening** to the new Coldplay CD.*

Unit 13

Prepositions of time: *at, in, on*

1   We use *at* with times, and with the word *night*.
    *The class starts **at nine o'clock**.*
    *I get up **at 6:30**.*
    *My uncle works **at night**.*

2   We use *in* with parts of the day (but not with *night*), and with months and seasons.
    *I go to school **in the morning**.*   *I often read **in the evening**.*
    *Her birthday is **in September**.*   *We go on vacation **in August**.*
    *It's always cold **in the winter**.*   *I like going to the beach **in the summer**.*

3   We use *on* with days of the week.
    *We have an English class **on Monday**.*   *I usually go to the movie theater **on Saturday**.*

Asking for permission: *Can I ...? / Yes, you can. / Sorry, you can't.*

1   We often use *Can I ...?* to ask for permission to do something.
    ***Can I** leave now, please?*   ***Can I** go to the party on Saturday?*

2   To give or refuse permission, we use *can* or *can't*.
    ***Can I** borrow your jacket?*
    *Yes, you **can**.   No, sorry, you **can't**. I want to wear it tonight.*

one/ones

We use *one* or *ones* when we don't want to repeat a noun. We use *one* instead of a singular noun and *ones* instead of a plural noun.
*My bicycle's very old. I want a new **one**. (= bicycle)*
*I have a CD by Muse, but it's an old **one**. (= CD)*
*I'd like two chocolate cupcakes and two strawberry **ones**. (= cupcakes)*
*Do you know those boys – the **ones** in the café? (= boys)*

Unit 14

Simple past: *was/wasn't; were/weren't*

1   We use the simple past form of *be* to talk about actions and events in the past.

2   We form the simple past like this:

I was	*we were*
he/she/it was	*you were*
	they were

I was in town on Saturday.   *He was tired after the game.*   *It was hot last week.*

You were late yesterday.   *We were at the movie theater last night.*   *They were angry.*

3   We make the negative by adding *not* (*was not, were not*). In speaking and informal writing we use short forms: *wasn't* and *weren't*.

I wasn't here last year.   *The movie wasn't interesting.*

You weren't at school yesterday.   *They weren't at the concert.*

4   To make questions, we put the verb before the subject.

Were you in town on Saturday?   *Was James happy about the test?*

5   We often use time expressions with the simple past.

yesterday   yesterday morning   yesterday afternoon   yesterday evening

last night   last Friday   last week   last weekend   last month   last year

Unit 15

Simple past: regular verbs

1   We use the simple past to talk about actions and events in the past.

2   With regular verbs we form the simple past by adding *-ed*. The form is the same for all subjects.

I walked to school yesterday.   *She opened the door.*   *The concert started at 8 o'clock.*

You finished before me.   *We played cards last night.*   *They watched the news on TV.*

3   If a verb ends with consonant + *y*, we change the *y* to *i* and add *-ed*.

study – studied   marry – married   carry – carried

If a short verb ends in 1 vowel + 1 consonant, we double the final consonant before adding *-ed*. We do the same if the verb ends in 1 vowel + l.

stop – stopped   hop – hopped

In American English, if a short verb ends in 1 vowel + *l*, we don't often double the final *l* before adding *-ed*.

travel – traveled   *cancel – canceled*

4   We make the negative with *didn't* (*did not*) + base form of the verb.

I didn't walk to school yesterday.   *She didn't open the door.*

You didn't finish before me.   *We didn't play cards last night.*

5   We make questions with *Did* + subject + base form of the verb.

Did I start before you?   *Did he open the window?*

Did you walk to school yesterday?   *Did they play volleyball last week?*

Simple past: irregular verbs

1   A lot of common verbs are irregular. This means that the simple past forms are different. They don't have the usual *-ed* ending.

go – went   see – saw   find – found   write – wrote   think – thought

There is a list of irregular verbs on page 117 of the Student's Book.

2   We make questions and negatives in the same way as for regular verbs.

I went downtown, but I didn't go to the bookstore.   *Did you go to the newsstand?*

We saw James, but we didn't see Jonathan.   *Did you see Alison?*

Unit 16

Comparative adjectives

1   To compare two things, or two groups of things, we use a comparative form + *than*.
    *I'm **older than** my brother.*
    *France is **bigger than** Britain.*
    *TVs are **more expensive than** radios.*
    *Your computer is **better than** mine.*

2   With short adjectives, we normally add -*er*.
    old – older   cheap – cheaper   quiet – quieter

    If the adjective ends in *e*, we add only -*r*.
    nice – nicer   safe – safer   free – freer

    If the adjective ends with consonant + *y*, we change the y to *i* and add -*er*.
    easy – easier   early – earlier   happy – happier

    If the adjective ends in 1 vowel + 1 consonant, we double the final consonant and add -*er*.
    big – bigger   sad – sadder   thin – thinner

3   With longer adjectives, we don't change the adjective – we put *more* in front of it.
    *expensive – **more** expensive   difficult – **more** difficult   interesting – **more** interesting*

4   Some adjectives are irregular – they have a different comparative form.
    *good – **better**   bad – **worse***

Notes

Notes

Notes

Notes

Notes

Notes

Notes

Thanks and acknowledgments

The authors would like to thank a number of people whose support has proved invaluable during the planning, writing and production process of *American English in Mind*.

First of all we would like to thank the numerous teachers and students in many countries of the world who have used the first edition of *English in Mind*. Their enthusiasm for the course, and the detailed feedback and valuable suggestions we got from many of them were an important source of inspiration and guidance for us in developing the concept and in the creation of *American English in Mind*.

In particular, the authors and publishers would like to thank the following teachers who gave up their valuable time for classroom observations, interviews and focus groups:

Brazil

Warren Cragg (ASAP Idiomas); Angela Pinheiro da Cruz (Colégio São Bento; Carpe Diem); Ana Paula Vedovato Maestrello (Colégio Beatíssima Virgem Maria); Natália Mantovanelli Fontana (Lord's Idiomas); Renata Condi de Souza (Colégio Rio Branco, Higienópolis Branch); Alexandra Arruda Cardoso de Almeida (Colégio Guilherme Dumont Villares / Colégio Emilie de Villeneuve); Gisele Siqueira (Speak Up); Ana Karina Giusti Mantovani (Idéia Escolas de Línguas); Maria Virgínia G. B. de Lebron (UFTM / private lessons); Marina Piccinato (Speak Up); Patrícia Nero (Cultura Inglesa / Vila Mariana); Graziela Barroso (Associação Alumni); Francisco Carlos Peinado (Wording); Maria Lúcia Sciamarelli (Colégio Divina Providencia / Jundiaí); Deborah Hallal Jorge (Nice Time Language Center); Lilian Itzicovitch Leventhal (Colégio I. L. Peretz); Dulcinéia Ferreira (One Way Línguas); and Priscila Prieto and Carolina Cruz Marques (Seven Idiomas).

Colombia

Luz Amparo Chacón (Gimnasio Los Monjes); Mayra Barrera; Diana de la Pava (Colegio de la Presentación Las Ferias); Edgar Ardila (Col. Mayor José Celestino Mutis); Sandra Cavanzo B. (Liceo Campo David); Claudia Susana Contreras and Luz Marína Zuluaga (Colegio Anglo Americano); Celina Roldán and Angel Torres (Liceo Cervantes del Norte); Nelson Navarro; Maritza Ruiz Martín; Francisco Mejía, and Adriana Villalba (Colegio Calasanz).

Ecuador

Paul Viteri (Colegio Andino, Quito); William E. Yugsan (Golden Gate Academy – Quito); Irene Costales (Unidad Educativa Cardinal Spellman Femenino); Vinicio Sanchez and Sandra Milena Rodríguez (Colegio Santo Domingo de Guzmán); Sandra Rigazio and María Elena Moncayo (Unidad Educativa Tomás Moro, Quito); Jenny Alexandra Jara Recalde and Estanislao Javier Pauta (COTAC, Quito); Verónica Landázuri and Marisela Madrid (Unidad Educativa "San Francisco de Sales"); Oswaldo Gonzalez and Monica Tamayo (Angel Polibio Chaves School, Quito); Rosario Llerena and Tania Abad (Isaac Newton, Quito); María Fernanda Mármol Mazzini and Luis Armijos (Unidad Educativa Letort, Quito); and Diego Bastidas and Gonzalo Estrella (Colegio Gonzaga, Quito).

Mexico

Connie Alvarez (Colegio Makarenko); Julieta Zelinski (Colegio Williams); Patricia Avila (Liceo Ibero Mexicano); Patricia Cervantes de Brofft (Colegio Frances del Pedregal); Alicia Sotelo (Colegio Simon Bolivar); Patricia Lopez (Instituto Mexico, A.C.); Maria Eugenia Fernandez Castro (Instituto Oriente Arboledas); Lilian Ariadne Lozano Bustos (Universidad Tecmilenio); Maria del Consuelo Contreras Estrada (Liceo Albert Einstein); Alfonso Rene Pelayo Garcia (Colegio Tomas Alva Edison); Ana Pilar Gonzalez (Instituto Felix de Jesus Rougier); and Blanca Kreutter (Instituto Simon Bolivar).

Our heartfelt thanks go to the *American English in Mind* team for their cooperative spirit, their many excellent suggestions and their dedication, which have been characteristic of the entire editorial process: Paul Phillips, Amy E. Hawley, Kelley Perrella, Eric Zuarino, Pam Harris, Kate Powers, Brigit Dermott, Kate Spencer, Heather McCarron, Keaton Babb, Roderick Gammon, Hugo Loyola, Howard Siegelman, Colleen Schumacher, Margaret Brooks, Kathryn O'Dell, Genevieve Kocienda, Lisa Hutchins, and Lynne Robertson.

We would also like to thank the teams of educational consultants, representatives and managers working for Cambridge University Press in various countries around the world. Space does not allow us to mention them all by name here, but we are extremely grateful for their support and their commitment.

In Student's Book 2, thanks go to David Crystal for the interview in Unit 9, and to Jon Turner for giving us the idea of using the story of Ulises de la Cruz in Unit 15.

Thanks to the team at Pentacor for giving the book its design; the staff at Full House Productions for the audio recordings; and Lightning Pictures for the video.

Last but not least, we would like to thank our partners, Mares and Adriana, for their support.

The publishers are grateful to the following illustrators:

Andrew Hennessey, Dan Chernett c/o Bright, Humberto c/o Sylvie Poggio, Mark Watkinson c/o Illustration, Mel Croft c/o Eye Candy, Mark Duffin, Nila Aye c/o New Division, Red Jelly, RobMcClurken, Rosa Dodd c/o Nb Illustration, Tracey Knight c/o Lemonade

The publishers are grateful to the following for permission to reproduce photographic material:

Key: l = left, c = center, r = right, t = top, b = bottom

Alamy/©blickwinkel p 68 (r), /©Louise Murray p 72 (b), /©Janine Wiedel Photolibrary pp 68 (l); Corbis/©DLILLC p 38, /©Emely p 56, /©Ada Summer p 36; / Taxi/Jim Cummins p 64 (5), / jashlock p 64 (1), /JulieJJ p 64 (6), /Sportstock p 64 (2); Photolibrary.com/Afl o Foto Agency p 64 (3), /Fresh Food Images/Joy Skipper p 72 (t), /imagebroker.net/Manfred Grebler p 64 (4), /White/Chase Jarvis p 64(8), /White/ Ryan McVay p 64 (7); Rex Features p 82, /Everett Collection/Wisconsin Historical Society p 86, /SNAP p 84; www.teamhoyt.com p 62.

Shutterstock/©Jim Parkin p 17 (tr), iStockphoto/©Galina Barskaya p 17 (cr), iStockphoto/©Christoph Riddle p 17 (br), iStockphoto/©digitalskillet p 18 (tr), iStockphoto/©Michael Krinke p 24 (tr), Getty Images/©Jo Hale p 24 (cr), iStockphoto/ ©Jose Manuel Gelpi Diaz p 47 (cl), Getty Images/©Michael Blann/Taxi p 54 (tl), iStockphoto/©Michael DeLeon p 60 (tr), Getty Images/©Glow Images p 72 (tr), Shutterstock/©Dustie/ Shutterstock p 77 (bl), Alamy/©Alex Segre p 78 (policeman), Getty Images/©Skip Nall/Photodisc p 78 (doorman), Ambient Images/©Frances M. Roberts p 78 (subway worker), Getty Images /©Image Source p 78 (business man), AP Photo/©George Gongora-Corpus Christi Caller-Times p 80 (cl), AP Photo/©PA, Myung Jung Kim p 80 (cr),

The publishers are grateful to the following for their assistance with commissioned photographs:

Alex Medeville